DANNY PROULX

DISPLAY CASES YOU CAN BUILD

**POPULAR
WOODWORKING
BOOKS**

CINCINNATI, OHIO
www.popularwoodworking.com

Read This Important Safety Notice

To prevent accidents, keep safety in mind while you work. The tool guards in some photos have been removed for clarity. Use the safety guards installed on power equipment; they are for your protection. When working on power equipment, keep fingers away from saw blades, wear safety goggles to prevent injuries from flying wood chips and sawdust, wear headphones to protect your hearing and consider installing a dust vacuum to reduce the amount of airborne sawdust in your woodshop. Don't wear loose clothing, such as neckties or shirts with loose sleeves, or jewelry, such as rings, necklaces or bracelets, when working on power equipment. Tie back long hair to prevent it from getting caught in your equipment. People who are sensitive to certain chemicals should check the chemical content of any product before using it. The authors and editors who compiled this book have tried to make the contents as accurate and correct as possible. Plans, illustrations, photographs and text have been carefully checked. All instructions, plans and projects should be carefully read, studied and understood before beginning construction. Due to the variability of local conditions, construction materials, skill levels, etc., neither the author nor Popular Woodworking Books assumes any responsibility for any accidents, injuries, damages or other losses incurred resulting from the material presented in this book. Prices listed for supplies and equipment were current at the time of publication and are subject to change. Glass shelving should have all edges polished and must be tempered. Untempered glass shelves may shatter and can cause serious bodily injury. Tempered shelves are very strong and if they break will just crumble, minimizing personal injury.

Metric Conversion Chart

TO CONVERT	TO	MULTIPLY BY
Inches	Centimeters	2.54
Centimeters	Inches	0.40
Feet	Centimeters	30.5
Centimeters	Feet	0.03
Yards	Meters	0.90
Meters	Yards	1.10
Sq. Inches	Sq. Centimeters	6.45
Sq. Centimeters	Sq. Inches	0.16
Sq. Feet	Sq. Meters	0.09
Sq. Meters	Sq. Feet	10.8
Sq. Yards	Sq. Meters	0.80
Sq. Meters	Sq. Yards	1.20
Pounds	Kilograms	0.45
Kilograms	Pounds	2.20
Ounces	Grams	28.3
Grams	Ounces	0.035

Display Cases You Can Build. Copyright © 2002 by Danny Proulx. Manufactured in Singapore. All rights reserved. No part of this book may be reproduced in any form or by any electronic or mechanical means, including information storage and retrieval systems, without permission in writing from the publisher, except by a reviewer, who may quote brief passages in a review. Published by Popular Woodworking Books, an imprint of F&W Publications, Inc., 4700 East Galbraith Road, Cincinnati, Ohio, 45236. First edition.

Visit our Web site at www.popularwoodworking.com for more information and resources for woodworkers.

Other fine Popular Woodworking Books are available from your local bookstore or direct from the publisher.

06   05   04   03   02   5   4   3   2   1

Library of Congress Cataloging-in-Publication Data

Proulx, Danny, 1947-
    Display cases you can build / by Danny Proulx.
      p. cm.
    Includes index.
    ISBN 1-55870-606-2 (alk. paper)
      1. Cabinetwork. 2. Shelving (Furniture) I. Title.

TT197 .P75965 2002
684.1'6--dc21

200219822

Editor: Jim Stack
Associate editor: Jennifer Ziegler
Content edited by Jennifer Churchill
Designed by Brian Roeth
Interior Layout by Cheryl VanDeMotter
Step-by-step photography by Danny Proulx
Production coordinated by Mark Griffin

Cover and chapter lead photography by Michael Bowie, Lux Photography, 2450 Lancaster Rd., Suite 25, Ottawa, Ont., Canada, 613-247-7199
Technical illustrations by Len Churchill, Lenmark Communications Ltd., 590 Alden Rd., Suite 206, Markham, Ont., Canada, 905-475-5222
Workshop site: Rideau Cabinets, P.O. Box 331, Russell, Ont., Canada K4R 1E1, 613-445-3722

Acknowledgements

Many suppliers have contributed products, material and technical support during the project-building phase of making this book. I appreciate how helpful they've been and recommend these companies without hesitation. Please see page 127 for more sources.

JULIUS BLUM INC.
800-438-6788
www.blum.com

DELTA MACHINERY
800-223-7278 (in US)
800-463-3582 (in Canada)
www.deltawoodworking.com

L.R.H. ENTERPRISES, INC.
800-423-2544
www.lrhent.com

JESSEM TOOL CO.
Rout-R-Slide
800-436-6799
www.jessem.com

About the Author

Danny Proulx has been involved in the woodworking field for more than 30 years and has operated a custom kitchen cabinet shop since 1989. He is a contributing editor to *CabinetMaker* magazine and has published articles in other magazines such as *Canadian Home Workshop*, *Canadian Woodworking*, *Popular Woodworking*, *WoodShop News*, and *Homes & Cottages*.

His earlier books include *Build Your Own Kitchen Cabinets*, *The Kitchen Cabinetmaker's Building and Business Manual*, *How to Build Classic Garden Furniture*, *Smart Shelving and Storage Solutions*, *Building Modern Cabinetry*, *Building More Classic Garden Furniture* and *Build Your Own Home Office Furniture*.

You can find Danny's Web site at www.cabinetmaking.com and he can be reached via e-mail by writing to danny@cabinetmaking.com.

Dedication

This book is another team effort. I couldn't meet deadlines, build and write without the dedicated help of my wife, Gale, and my shop assistant, Jack Chaters. The master of photographic art, Michael Bowie of Lux Photography in Ottawa, is the creator and adviser for all photographic images. Len Churchill, of Lenmark Communications in Markham, created the exploded views. Len is the best woodworking illustrator I've worked with and is a genius with an electronic pen.

The staff at Popular Woodworking Books is my support team and I'm very lucky to have such a talented and dedicated group of professionals. The PW team includes Jim Stack, Jennifer Churchill, Brian Roeth, Mark Griffin, Jennifer Ziegler and a dozen other stars. Thank you all for making my passion a true pleasure.

table of contents

introduction

When it comes to woodworking, there are a couple of basic principles I try to follow. First, I want to make use of the man-made materials that have been developed from wood. I prefer sheet material over solid wood because many sheet materials have been created using the so-called "garbage" woods. Scrub trees, stumps and timber that couldn't be used for boards in the past are now being made into particleboard or plycore sheets. Since it isn't being plowed under, burned or left to rot, our forests benefit.

One premium-grade log can be used for veneers, and the previously wasted trees make up the stable core. That beautiful lumber then becomes dozens of cabinets instead of just one. That's what I call extending a natural resource.

The second principle has to do with teaching and writing. I build cabinets, teach woodworking and write books. The teaching aspect must be the primary focus of each book. I don't write books to show everyone how much I know about the subject — that's not, nor should it be — the function of any book. It's a learning tool and must be created with that in mind. I hope I've accomplished that goal.

I realized a long time ago how little I know about this vast and wonderful world we call woodworking. I learn new things each day and try to pass them on to fellow woodworkers. I look forward to writing a book or teaching a woodworking class because I know I will learn something new. That's the exciting and wonderful part of my work.

The projects I've designed and built for this book illustrate different techniques. I've attempted to show a number of ways to build a carcass, door and drawer. Almost all the projects have doors, but they are built using different techniques in an attempt to show different methods and styles of joinery. Don't be shy about using a technique in one chapter to build a project in another — that's the whole idea. Don't hesitate to experiment, because the knowledge gained by making mistakes is valuable.

Finally, as I've said in other books, you can build any of these projects simply by following the plans. As a result you'll have a nice piece of furniture that will last a few years. However, the real value is learning something new.

hardware, materials and joinery

I DON'T LIKE TO FILL A LOT OF pages with tool pictures and basic woodworking information — this is a project book! But I will detail a few of the products, tools and terms I use throughout this book to aid you in following the project steps.

The materials I use are modern sheet goods and hardwoods. I prefer using veneer-covered particleboards and plywood cores because of their stability. When properly built, a cabinet made with modern sheet material is strong and stable.

Today's hardware has kept pace with the development of sheet goods. There are special screws, drawer slides, hinges and dozens of other joinery aids that are easy to use and mechanically secure. I'll detail a few of the most important items in the next few pages.

Joinery procedures have remained unchanged for decades. The mortise and tenon, rabbet, dado, finger and dovetail joints continue to be used on a daily basis. There are some new techniques to implement when you use these old standards with new materials, but for the most part the techniques are the same.

New methods, such as pocket-hole and biscuit joinery, have made an appearance. These two joinery systems are excellent alternatives and have been widely accepted by woodworkers.

I'll detail both the old and new joinery methods, and try to use different techniques with each project. You can pick the project and use any of the procedures detailed to build your own version. I'll also show you a few door-making techniques that can be used on dozens of cabinet applications. And don't miss out on building any of these projects because you haven't got a few fancy tools. There are alternatives to each step in the process, so pick one that suits your abilities, needs and the tools you own.

hardware

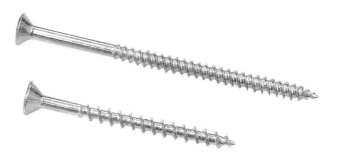

There are thousands of new hardware items available to meet the needs of woodworkers. Many have been developed for the commercial furniture industry and adapted for home woodworkers. In this chapter I'll detail a few of the most important items. You'll find descriptions and procedures throughout the book whenever a new piece of hardware is introduced.

1 | One of the most important hardware items is the particleboard (PB) screw. Compare it to a standard wood screw, shown at the top in the photo, and you'll notice a few differences. First, the shaft is thinner on the PB screw. Second, the threads are coarse, which provides a superior grip in particleboard, medium-density fiberboard or plycore material. However, the PB screw design will fail unless a proper pilot hole is drilled. I don't agree with any manufacturer that suggests a pilot hole isn't necessary for their screws. Without the hole, a screw acts like a wedge and damages the board.

2 | A lot of hardware items are designed specifically for glass. These include hinges, latches and handles. In some cases the glass will require drilling, which is a service local glass suppliers offer. Remember when working with glass that all exposed edges must be polished. And all glass used for shelving should be tempered. Again, this is a service offered by your supplier on request.

SAFETY IN THE SHOP

Safety means using common sense and not working when you're tired or distracted. It also means using all of your protective equipment when working in a potentially dangerous environment. Hearing and eyesight are not easily replaced, so take the time to work safely.

3 Adjustable shelf pins in ordinary kitchen cabinets are plain and functional. Display cabinets expose these pins so a more decorative type is often used. The pins shown here are brass, with brass sleeves for the holes. The punch, shown at the top of the photo, is needed to drive the sleeves into the holes.

tip

parts of a hinge

The two-part hidden hinge, which is mounted on both the door and the mounting plate, is attached to the cabinet side or gable end of the cabinet. The hinge body is attached to the mounting plate with a screw or a clip pin. The clip-on method is becoming popular because you can remove the door from the mounting plate without disturbing the adjustments you've already made.

4 Another style of adjustable shelf hardware makes use of a metal strip and pins. These strips are often installed in grooves cut into the cabinet sides.

5 In the last few years door-mounting hardware from Europe has become a very popular alternative. The so-called "European hidden hinge" is now widely used as standard kitchen cabinet door hardware. The hidden hinge usually requires a 35mm hole drilled in the door. That task seems a bit challenging to some people, but it's a straightforward process. There is a learning curve when working with the hidden hinge. For instance, these hinges are classified with terms such as full overlay and half overlay. These terms simply refer to the distance the door covers the cabinet side member (gable end). The third type of hinge is an inset style that is used to mount the doors flush with the cabinet face.

tip

degrees of opening

Hidden hinges are also classed in terms of "degrees of opening." For standard door applications, the 100° to 110° hinges are common, but you can purchase hinges that will allow the door to open from 90° to 170°. The term simply refers to the number of degrees of swing that the door can open from its closed position.

materials

1 | Wood veneer sheet material is the product of choice for modern cabinetry. Only the best-quality wood is used to make veneers. These thin sheets of wood are bonded to many different substrates to make cabinet-grade sheet goods. The materials shown in this photo are, from left to right, plywood, multicore board and particleboard. All are covered with high-grade oak veneer.

2 | Combining solid wood and modern sheet material is common practice at most cabinet shops. Here melamine particleboard is edged with oak hardwood.

3 | Just about every cabinet in your home that was built in the last 20 years uses a combination of natural and man-made materials. Kitchen, bathroom, bedroom and family room cabinets are often made using sheet material and hardwood. The cabinets pictured in this illustration were built with melamine particleboard interiors and drawers. The raised-panel doors and drawer fronts are made of maple.

joinery

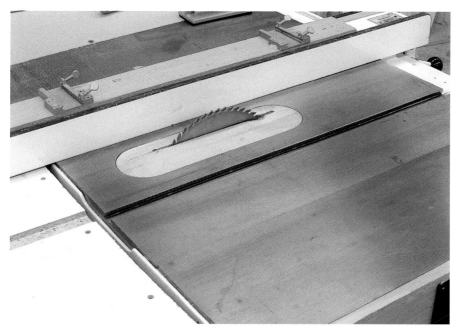

1 Joining wood can be done by hand — that's the way it was done in the past and there's nothing wrong with a good, handmade joint. Today many of us rely on power tools, and the most important of these is the table saw. Spending a few extra dollars for a good-quality saw is a wise investment. Keep it well tuned and you'll be able to meet any woodworking challenge.

2 Plate joinery is often called biscuit joinery. Slots are cut with a special tool in the two pieces of material that are to be joined. Glue and a beechwood biscuit are put in the slots and the two pieces are clamped together. The glue dries to form a bond and the water in the glue swells the biscuit creating a tighter grip. It is a great joinery method and one that's used throughout this book. The biscuits are available in three sizes. No. 0 is the smallest, No. 10 is the middle size and No. 20 is the largest. You may come across "mini" biscuits, which are smaller than the No. 0 and are used for applications such as joining 45° miters on picture frames.

3 I believe pilot holes are necessary when installing screw fasteners. The shaft of a screw is a wedge, and unless you remove the material occupied by the shaft, the board will likely split. Drill a hole equal to the screw's shaft size and the threads will be properly cut. That's how you'll achieve maximum grip and a mechanically sound connection. Invest in a good-quality carbide drill counterbore combination bit. The counterbore portion removes waste for the screw head and, if it's a 3/8"-diameter model, will bore holes for standard wood plugs at the same time.

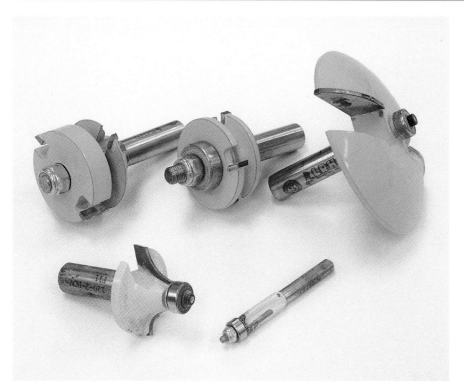

4 After the table saw, the router is the next most important tool in your shop. These tools, in combination with the hundreds of bits available, can create joinery cuts, profiles, mouldings and trim. The green set of bits in the photo are used to make raised-panel doors. The yellow bit on the left is a standard roundover bit and the one on the right is a flush-trim bit. It's both wise and cost effective to purchase the highest quality carbide-tipped bits available. The best bits can be sharpened many times, and the carbide models won't burn when cutting through the high glue content in man-made materials.

GROOVE

RABBET

DADO

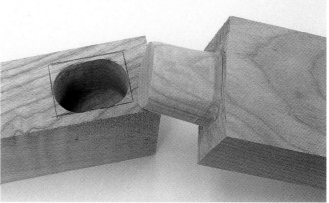

6 One of the oldest and most reliable woodworking joints is the mortise and tenon. It can be made with a square hole and square tenon or a rounded version, as shown in this photo.

5 Joinery terminology is sometimes confusing and often incorrectly applied by even the most experienced woodworkers. In this book, a dado is a channel cut across the grain in a board. A groove is a channel along the board's grain and a rabbet is an open-sided channel on the end or side of the material.

7 The box or finger joint is another popular method used for building drawer boxes. It has many applications and is mechanically secure, as well as decorative. This joint can be cut by hand, on a table saw or with a router in a table. It's simple to make and is often used in circumstances where the joint will be visible.

8 This tenon-and-groove joint is used for door frames and panels. It's a strong joint, and one that is used a great deal throughout this book.

9 Pocket-hole joinery is a recent addition to the woodworker's joinery options. The slot is cut with a jig, and a special screw is installed to secure the pieces. You will need a special jig and drill bit with the proper screws if you want to use this joint, but it is well worth the investment.

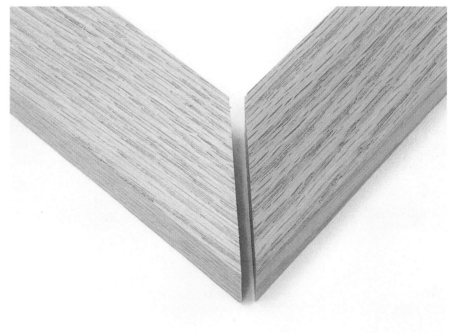

10 We will be using a few different variations of the standard miter joint. The most common is a 90° corner that requires both pieces to be cut at 45°. The cuts can be made by hand, but using a power miter box seems to be the most popular method. A basic power miter or "chop" saw isn't expensive, particularly if you will use it often in your shop.

table display cabinet

WHILE RESEARCHING THIS book I discovered the importance of handmade dolls, antique guns, figurines and models like the ship shown at the right.

Almost everybody collects something. I didn't realize how many collectibles are sitting on a shelf or dining room sideboard and are suffering from potential damage because they are unprotected. A number of these beautiful collectibles are not displayed because their owners fear they might be damaged, but I believe I have found a solution in this display cabinet.

This beautiful handmade scale model of the racing schooner *Bluenose* was crafted by the late Stanley Gosling Sr. of Sydney, Nova Scotia. All of the fittings were built by Mr. Gosling, including the sails and rigging.

The schooner *Bluenose* was built and launched in Lunenburg, Nova Scotia, in 1921. In October 1921, after a season fishing on the Grand Banks, *Bluenose* defeated Gloucester's *Elsie* and brought the International Fisherman's trophy home. In an 18-year racing career, *Bluenose* did not give up the trophy.

For more information on the Web about this schooner and its new life as *Bluenose II* go to www.bluenose2.ns.ca.

This enclosed case offers a number of benefits to the collector. The item can be seen from all sides, but is well protected from dust and dirt. The design also prevents accidental handling of those fragile pieces. There are no doors; the only access is from the top.

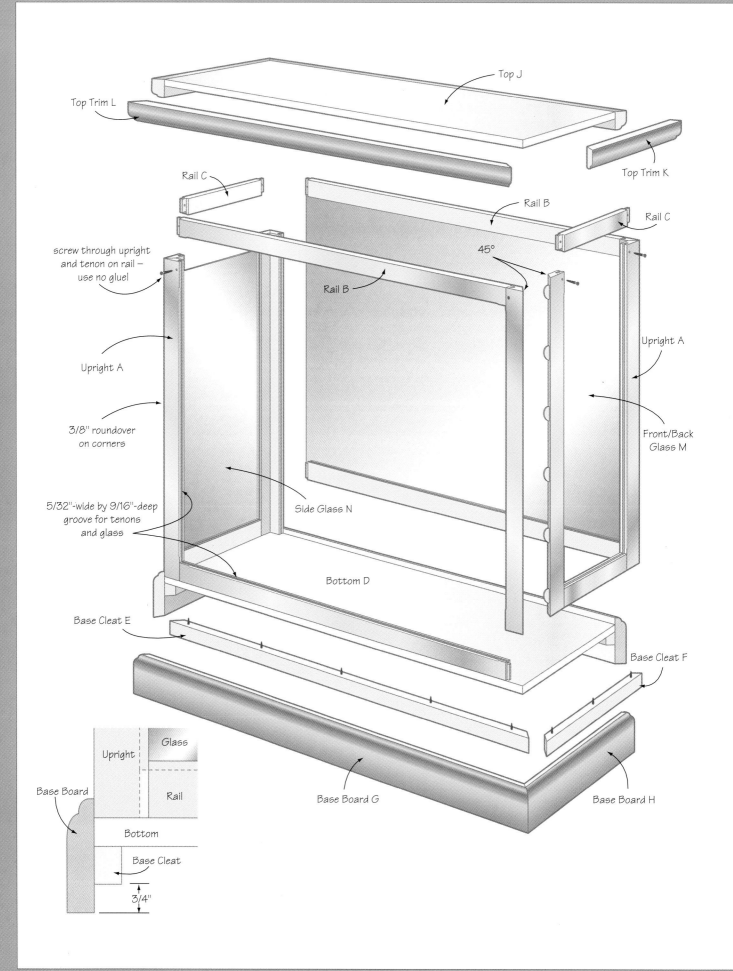

Top J

Top Trim L

Top Trim K

Rail C

Rail B

Rail C

screw through upright
and tenon on rail –
use no glue!

45°

Upright A

Rail B

Upright A

3/8" roundover
on corners

Front/Back
Glass M

5/32"-wide by 9/16"-deep
groove for tenons
and glass

Side Glass N

Bottom D

Base Cleat E

Base Cleat F

Glass

Upright

Rail

Base Board

Bottom

Base Cleat

Base Board G

Base Board H

3/4"

materials list | **inches**

REFERENCE	QUANTITY	PART	STOCK	THICKNESS	WIDTH	LENGTH	COMMENTS
A	8	uprights	oak	3/4	1 1/2	30	
B	4	rails	oak	3/4	1 1/2	34	
C	4	rails	oak	3/4	1 1/2	9	
D	1	bottom	oak plywood	3/4	11	36	
E	2	base cleats	oak	3/4	1	34 1/2	
F	2	base cleats	oak	3/4	1	11	
G	2	base boards	oak	3/4	3	37 1/2	
H	2	base boards	oak	3/4	3	12 1/2	
J	1	top	oak plywood	3/4	11	36	
K	2	top trim	oak	3/4	1 1/2	12 1/2	
L	2	top trim	oak	3/4	1 1/2	37 1/2	
M	2	front & back	glass	1/8	28	34	
N	2	sides	glass	1/8	28	9	

materials list | **millimeters**

REFERENCE	QUANTITY	PART	STOCK	THICKNESS	WIDTH	LENGTH	COMMENTS
A	8	uprights	oak	19	38	762	
B	4	rails	oak	19	38	864	
C	4	rails	oak	19	38	229	
D	1	bottom	oak plywood	19	279	914	
E	2	base cleats	oak	19	25	877	
F	2	base cleats	oak	19	25	279	
G	2	base boards	oak	19	76	962	
H	2	base boards	oak	19	76	318	
J	1	top	oak plywood	19	279	914	
K	2	top trim	oak	19	38	318	
L	2	top trim	oak	19	38	962	
M	2	front & back	glass	3	711	864	
N	2	sides	glass	3	711	229	

1 Cut all the uprights and rails A, B and C. Use the table saw, or router table with an appropriate bit, to make a groove on one long edge of each piece. The grooves must be centered and should all be 5/32"-wide by 9/16"-deep.

2 Each rail requires a tenon, centered on both ends, that's 5/32"-thick by 1/2"-long. Use your table saw and miter gauge to cut the rail tenons.

3 Cut a 45° angle on the long edge, opposite the grooved edge, of each upright. Set the table saw blade to 45° and make a few test cuts. The widest face of each upright, after completing the cut, should be 1½" wide. Or, if you'd like to use an alternative method for making the posts try the following: Avoid cutting the uprights, as well as the joinery in the next step, by using 1½"-square stock for the uprights. All that's required is a ¾"-square rabbet cut on one corner of each post. Make the glass grooves in each post, as detailed in step 1.

4 Join two uprights to form a corner post. Join the remaining uprights to create the four corner posts. Use glue and four No. 0 biscuits per joint to build the posts. Angle the plate joiner and place your cuts in an area that won't interfere with the glass grooves.

5 Begin the frame assembly by attaching two corner posts and the short rails. Glue and clamp the bottom rail in place, making sure the glass grooves are aligned with each other. Do not apply glue to the top rails, as they must be removed to change and install the glass panels. The top rails will be secured later.

6 Once the two end frames are secure, join them by installing the front and rear lower rails. Apply glue and clamp securely.

8 The bottom board D is attached to the frame with glue and 1½"-long screws. Align the board so it's flush with the outside faces of the rails and uprights.

7 The upper rails cannot be glued in place. Drill a small pilot hole ½" below the top edge, through the upright and into each tenon. Countersink these holes so the screw head will be flush with the wood surface. Carefully install ⅝"-long screws in these holes to secure the rails.

tip

I am using ⅛"-thick glass so the grooves will be 5/32" wide to ensure an easy fit. Verify your actual glass thickness before cutting the grooves.

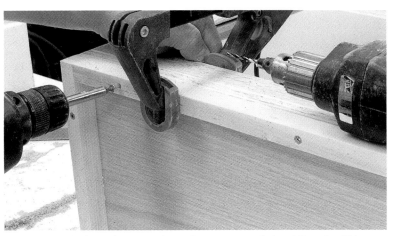

9 Now is an ideal time to finish sand the cabinet. Use a ³⁄₈"-radius roundover bit in a router to round over the outside face on the inside perimeter of each frame opening.

10 Attach the base cleats E and F with 2" screws and glue. They should be aligned flush with the outside edge of the bottom board.

11 Use the same ³⁄₈"-radius roundover bit to ease the outside corners of each upright. Stop the cuts ³⁄₄" from the bottom and top edge of each upright.

12 The measurements for the base boards G and H are on the longest face after the 45° cut has been made. Before cutting these boards, verify the measurements on your cabinet. My base boards have a cove cut with a slightly rounded profile on the top outside edge. You can use the cove and roundover bit to make this cut, or cut a decorative profile to suit your taste. Apply glue and secure the four boards with 1¹⁄₄" screws through the base cleats into the backs of these base boards. Attach them so their bottom edge is ³⁄₄" below the lower edge of the base cleats E and F.

13 The top board J is ¾"-thick veneer plywood, to which the hardwood top trim K and L is attached. Use glue and biscuits or finishing nails to secure the trim. The hardwood top trim is mounted flush with the top face of board J. It should be ¾" below the bottom surface of J. All corners are mitered at 45°. Once they are secure, ease the sharp corners with a belt sander.

construction NOTES

This display case was finished with three coats of oil-based polyurethane. I gave it a final rub with #0000 steel wool and clear floor wax to get a smooth and hard glossy finish.

If your glass panels are loose, squeeze a small amount of clear silicone between the glass and upright, inside the groove. The silicone will dry clear and can be cut out if a glass panel requires changing.

Not everyone will need a case based on my dimensions. In fact, I'm sure no two cases will be the same size. To alter the cabinet size, adjust the rail lengths and post heights. All the remaining procedures will be identical.

The glass panels are expensive, so do a bit of comparison shopping. If your case is on a table with its back against a wall, you might want to substitute the back glass for a thin piece of veneer plywood to reduce the material cost.

There are a number of other options that can be installed in your display case. For instance, small "puck" lights can be attached to the underside of the top, and the power cord can be routed through the back corner post, then down the rear face.

If you need added security, the top can be attached with decorative screws on both end edges into the top rails.

The final touch for your display case might be the addition of a mirror covering the bottom board. For display collectibles such as this ship, a mirrored bottom adds a touch of class.

14 The bottom edge of the hardwood trim on the top board has the same decorative profile as the base boards. The top edge is a simple round over using a ⅜"-radius bit.

15 Verify your glass measurements. I ordered my panels ⅛" smaller than the width and height to allow for any wood movement. Test fit the panels, then remove them to apply a finish.

tall display cabinet

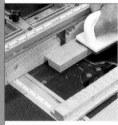

This cabinet is ideal for someone who has a collection of figurines or models. Equipped with lights and a glass panel door, it offers easy viewing and ample protection for your collection.

I BUILT THIS CABINET USING oak veneer multi-core plywood and solid wood. However, it can be made with any wood that matches your décor.

The lights, glass shelves and glass panel door combine to make this a beautiful and functional cabinet. The high cost of glass can be an important consideration, so I suggest you call your local glass supplier for a quote before starting this project.

Biscuit joinery is used extensively in this project. It's the ideal choice when joining solid wood to sheet material. If you haven't invested in a biscuit joiner, you're missing out on a great tool.

The glass panel door was built using a mortise-and-tenon joint, and the glass panels have been

set in a rabbet and secured with wood strips.

One of the best features of this project is the glass shelves. They can be adjusted to suit any collection, but more importantly, they allow the lights to illuminate every part of the cabinet.

This project can be built with or without a door. The cabinet looks and functions beautifully either way. The door offers an extra degree of security and provides more dust protection for your valuables.

The beauty and function of this cabinet is obvious when used to display collectibles, such as these Capodimonte figures, which are owned by the author.

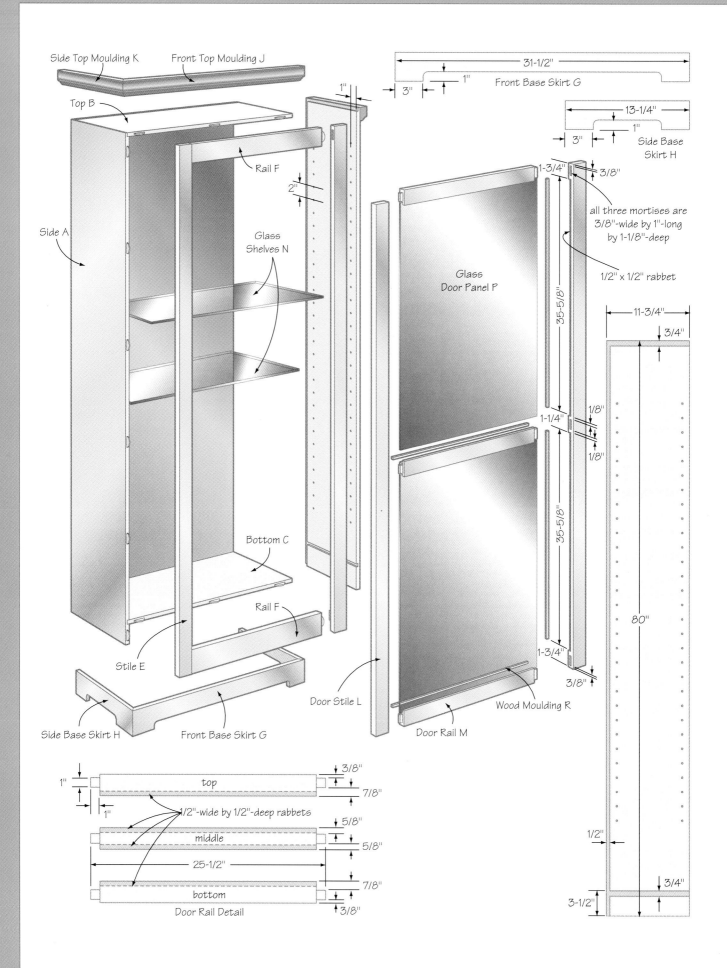

Side Top Moulding K

Front Top Moulding J

Top B

Side A

Rail F

2"

Glass Shelves N

Bottom C

Stile E

Rail F

Side Base Skirt H

Front Base Skirt G

1"

31-1/2"

3" 1"

Front Base Skirt G

13-1/4"

3" 1"

Side Base Skirt H

1-3/4"

3/8"

all three mortises are
3/8"-wide by 1"-long
by 1-1/8"-deep

1/2" x 1/2" rabbet

Glass
Door Panel P

35-5/8"

1-1/4"

1/8"

1/8"

35-5/8"

Door Stile L

Door Rail M

Wood Moulding R

1-3/4"

3/8"

11-3/4"

3/4"

80"

1/2"

3/4"

3-1/2"

3/8"

1"

top

7/8"

1"

1/2"-wide by 1/2"-deep rabbets

5/8"

middle

5/8"

25-1/2"

7/8"

bottom

3/8"

Door Rail Detail

materials list | **inches**

REFERENCE	QUANTITY	PART	STOCK	THICKNESS	WIDTH	LENGTH	COMMENTS
A	2	sides	oak plywood	$3/4$	$11^3/4$	80	
B	1	top	oak plywood	$3/4$	$11^1/4$	$29^1/2$	
C	1	bottom	oak plywood	$3/4$	$11^1/4$	$29^1/2$	
D	1	back board	oak particleboard	$1/2$	$29^1/2$	$77^1/4$	
E	2	stiles	oak	$3/4$	$1^1/2$	80	
F	2	rails	oak	$3/4$	$3^1/2$	27	
G	1	front base skirt	oak	$3/4$	3	$31^1/2$	angle cut on both ends
H	2	side base skirts	oak	$3/4$	3	$13^1/4$	angle cut on one end
J	1	front top moulding	oak	$3/4$	1	$31^1/2$	angle cut
K	2	side top mouldings	oak	$3/4$	1	$13^1/4$	angle cut
L	2	door stiles	oak	$3/4$	$2^1/4$	75	
M	3	door rails	oak	$3/4$	$2^1/4$	$25^1/2$	
N	5	shelves	glass	$1/4$	11	$28^3/8$	tempered with polished edges
P	2	door panels	glass	$1/8$	$24^3/8$	$35^1/8$	
Q	4	wood mouldings	oak	$3/8$	$3/8$	36	rough length
R	4	wood mouldings	oak	$3/8$	$3/8$	25	rough length

materials list | **millimeters**

REFERENCE	QUANTITY	PART	STOCK	THICKNESS	WIDTH	LENGTH	COMMENTS
A	2	sides	oak plywood	19	298	2032	
B	1	top	oak plywood	19	285	750	
C	1	bottom	oak plywood	19	285	750	
D	1	back board	oak particleboard	13	750	1962	
E	2	stiles	oak	19	38	2032	
F	2	rails	oak	19	89	686	
G	1	front base skirt	oak	19	76	800	angle cut on both ends
H	2	side base skirts	oak	19	76	336	angle cut on one end
J	1	front top moulding	oak	19	25	800	angle cut
K	2	side top mouldings	oak	19	25	336	angle cut
L	2	door stiles	oak	19	57	1905	
M	3	door rails	oak	19	57	648	
N	5	shelves	glass	6	279	721	tempered with polished edges
P	2	door panels	glass	3	620	892	
Q	4	wood mouldings	oak	10	10	914	rough length
R	4	wood mouldings	oak	10	10	635	rough length

1 | Prepare the two sides A by cutting the dadoes and rabbets as shown in the diagram. Use a ½" router bit in a table or with a guide bar if you're cutting the joints with a handheld router. Note that the rabbet on top, as well as the dado for the bottom shelf, is ½" wide. The back edge rabbet is only ½" wide.

2 | Drill two columns of holes on the inside face of each side panel for the adjustable shelf pins. Purchase the pins before drilling the holes to determine the exact size required. Make a jig with scrap lumber, spacing the holes about 2" apart. Drill the hole columns 1" in from each edge.

4 | I used ½"-thick veneer particleboard in place of the normal ¼" back board to add strength to this tall cabinet. Apply glue to the rabbets and nail the panel from the back side. Be sure to cut this board accurately so it will square the cabinet when installed.

3 | Cut and install the top and bottom boards B and C. They are attached flush with the front edges of each side. The top board can be glued and nailed in place because trim will cover the nail holes. The bottom board C must be attached with glue applied to the dadoes and clamped until set.

5 Install one stile E flush with the outside face of the side panel. It can be attached with glue and nails, or with glue and biscuits.

6 Attach the upper and lower rails F using glue and biscuits. Use one biscuit to secure each rail to the stile and three more to attach them to the top and bottom boards. The top edge of the bottom rail should be flush with the top surface of the bottom board.

7 Now install the remaining stile E with glue and biscuits. Attach it so its outside edge is flush with the outside face of the side board. If you don't own a biscuit joiner, attach the stiles and rails with glue and nails or dowels.

8 The base skirt consists of three pieces, G and H, as detailed in the Materials List. They are joined with 45° miters at each corner. Before cutting the miters, use a cove bit in your router to detail the top edge of each piece. Cutting the cove detail before the miters results in crisp corners on the skirt. Cut the pattern as shown and sand smooth.

9 Attach the three skirt boards to the case. The top edge of the skirt boards is secured 1¾" above the bottom edge of the side boards. Apply glue and attach the boards using 1¼" screws. Drive two screws into the back of each side skirt and four into the front skirt board.

10 The top moulding J and K can be any style. Pick a pattern that matches the furniture in the room where this case will be used. I've chosen a pattern that matches the cove detail on the skirt boards. Use glue and brad nails to secure the moulding.

11 Use a ⅜"-radius roundover bit in a router to ease the outside corners of each stile L. The router will stop when it hits the upper trim and lower skirt, determining the cut length.

tip

The door is 28"-wide by 75"-high. It will overlap the top and bottom rail by 1". The overlap design determines the door height. The door width, when using European or hidden hinges, can be easily calculated for this or any other cabinet. Measure the interior dimension of the cabinet and add 1" to that figure. That is the width of a door for this cabinet. If you require two doors, simply divide the calculated inside measurement by 2. For example, the inside measurement of this cabinet is 27". By adding 1" to the dimension I'll need one 28"-wide door or two 14"-wide doors.

12 Prepare the door stiles by cutting two rabbets ½"-wide by ½"-deep in each one. Stop the rabbets 1¾" from each end and leave a 1¼" uncut area at the center of each rail, M. The rabbets can be cut with a straight bit in a router table. Plunge the bit into each stile 1¾" from each end. The round corners left by the bit will be squared once the door frame is assembled.

13 | Use a drill press to remove most of the waste for the mortises in each stile. Clean out the remainder with a sharp chisel. The mortise is ⅜"-wide by 1⅛"-deep and 1"-long. Refer to the illustration for the correct locations of these mortises.

14 | The upper and lower rails require a ½"-wide by ½"-deep rabbet on one long edge. The middle rail requires the same rabbet cut on both long edges, as shown.

16 | Round over the square corners on each rail tenon so they'll fit properly in the mortises. Use a wood file to take off a little at a time, then test fit the joint. Once all the tenons are correct, assemble the doorframe with glue and clamps.

15 | Form the tenons on both ends of each rail, paying attention to their positions on the end and middle rails. The tenons are cut ⅜"-thick to fit tightly in the stile mortises. Use a table saw and miter fence to nibble away the waste and form the tenons. Or, if you have a tenoning jig, make the cheek cut and complete the tenons with the jig.

17 Once the glue has set and the joints are secure, square the corners of each rabbet on the doorframe. Use a sharp chisel on all eight corners.

18 Now is the best time to completely sand the doorframe. Use a ⅜"-radius roundover bit to ease the front outside edges of the door.

19 Verify your measurements before ordering the glass door panels and shelves. Rough cut the ⅜"-square wood moulding strips Q and R to length. They will be cut to the proper size and used to retain the glass door panels.

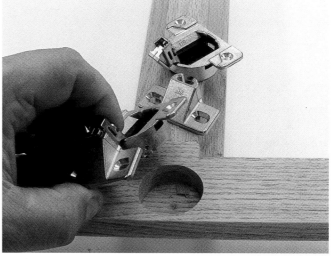

20 Drill three 35mm-diameter holes in the door for the hinges. The holes are ⅛" from the door edge and deep enough to properly seat the hinges. I used a hidden hinge with a plate designed for face frame mounting. The hinges are Blum Compact 33 series with a ½" overlay mounting plate. Apply the final finish now, as the best possible time is before the hardware and glass is installed. I used three coats of semigloss polyurethane to finish my case.

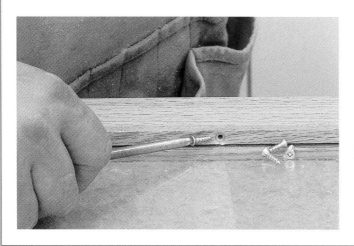

21 Set the glass panels P in place on the door. Use the ⅜" wood strips to retain the glass and secure the strips with ⅝"-long screws. Drill holes in the wood strips for each screw, so they will be drawn tight to the doorframe.

22 Install the hinges on the door. Mount the door to the cabinet by holding it in its open position with a ⅛"-thick strip of wood between the door and face frame. Secure the mounting plate.

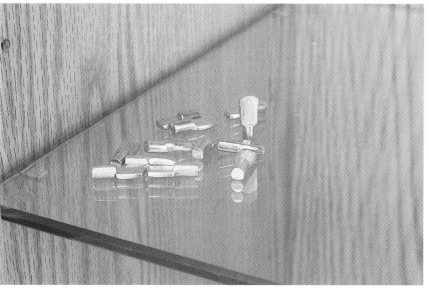

23 Brass pins that require a ³⁄₁₆"-diameter hole support the tempered glass shelves N. The edges on these shelves must be polished for safety reasons.

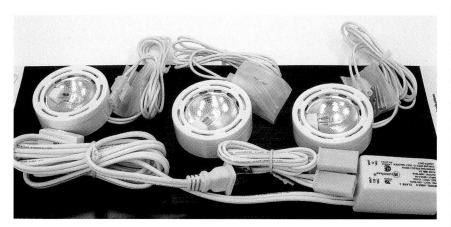

24 This cabinet was equipped with quartz halogen lights. Kits, such as the one shown, can be purchased at hardware stores or home centers.

construction NOTES

The cost of this project will be dramatically reduced if you don't require a door. But if you want a secure environment for your collection, and a bit more protection against dust, a door is the solution.

I didn't want attention drawn to the door, so I didn't install a handle. If you will be opening the door frequently, you may want to install one.

Installing a barrel lock on the door can further protect your collectibles. It won't stop a determined thief, but it will prevent excessive handling of your valuable collection. These inexpensive locks are available at hardware stores and home centers.

The cabinet is surprisingly stable and will stand unsupported. However, if there are small children in the home you might consider securing the case to the wall with a 3" screw through the back board into the wall stud.

I usually use red oak and apply three coats of polyurethane to most of my projects. The oak machines easily and is plentiful in my region, but any wood will work with this project. Choose a species that matches the other furniture in the room.

Biscuit joinery is an important part of this project, but as I previously stated, face nailing and glue or dowels are perfectly acceptable. Remember, there are dozens of ways to join wood, so find a method that suits your budget and experience.

The amount of material removed to form the rabbets is substantial. Where possible, make a series of small cuts instead of one large cut. It's a great deal safer and the results are often much better.

The doorframe is made with mortises and tenons, and the glass is secured with wood strips. Once again, there are a number of door construction options that I will detail in this book, and any of them can be used with this project.

wall-mounted cabinet

WALL SHELVES OFTEN LOOK like simple boxes that have been thrown together. The challenge is to design a functional shelf and keep it simple, while adding a little visual interest as well. I think that I have accomplished that goal by using a half-lap joint at the corners.

The shelves are adjustable and made of tempered glass to let light into every corner. The glass appears almost invisible so only the collection pieces are seen. That's an important point when displaying small items; some wall shelves overpower the collection.

This display shelf was built without doors, but you can install them if there is a requirement. I will discuss a few door options in the construction steps.

Keep this shelf in mind as a teaching project for a young woodworker. Not only can it be built with hand tools, it also illustrates the mechanical strength and usefulness of a half-lap joint. The edges can be formed with hand sanding, and the rabbets can be cut with a plane. Youngsters will love building this project and can always use a wall shelf in their room.

Wall shelves, such as this one, are in demand. Be prepared to build a few more when you show this project to family and friends.

The salt and pepper shaker collection shown here is owned by Elsa Cawthray of Ottawa, Ontario.

This is one of the simplest projects in this book, and it's one you'll probably build many times over. It seems that just about every collector has a number of small items that could be displayed on a wall shelf like this one.

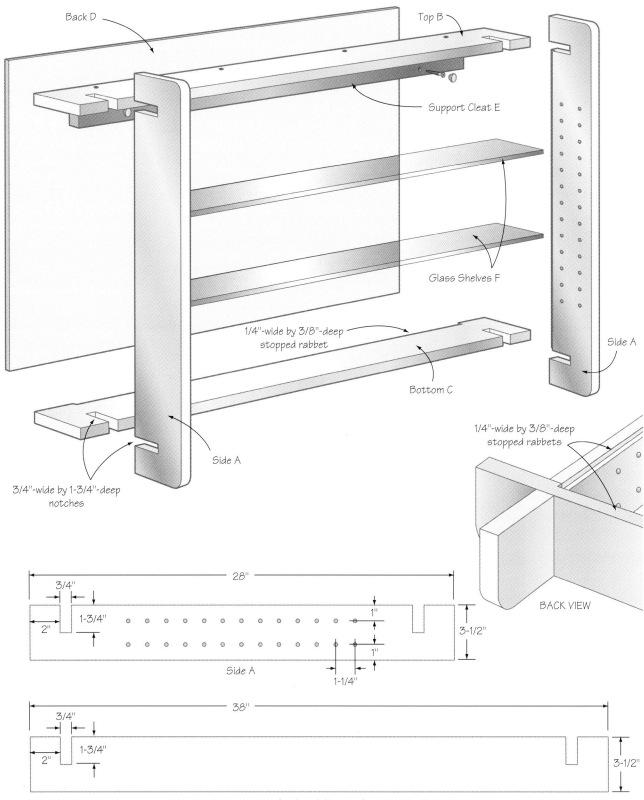

Back D

Top B

Support Cleat E

Glass Shelves F

Side A

1/4"-wide by 3/8"-deep
stopped rabbet

Bottom C

1/4"-wide by 3/8"-deep
stopped rabbets

Side A

3/4"-wide by 1-3/4"-deep
notches

BACK VIEW

28"

3/4"

1-3/4"

2"

1"

1"

3-1/2"

1-1/4"

Side A

38"

3/4"

1-3/4"

2"

3-1/2"

Top B and Bottom C

materials list | **inches**

REFERENCE	QUANTITY	PART	STOCK	THICKNESS	WIDTH	LENGTH	COMMENTS
A	2	sides	oak	3/4	3 1/2	28	
B	1	top	oak	3/4	3 1/2	38	
C	1	bottom	oak	3/4	3 1/2	38	
D	1	back board	oak	1/4	23 1/4	33 1/4	
E	1	support cleat	oak	3/4	1	32 1/2	
F	3	shelves	glass	1/4	3 1/4	32 7/16	

materials list | **millimeters**

REFERENCE	QUANTITY	PART	STOCK	THICKNESS	WIDTH	LENGTH	COMMENTS
A	2	sides	oak	19	89	711	
B	1	top	oak	19	89	965	
C	1	bottom	oak	19	89	965	
D	1	back board	oak	6	590	844	
E	1	support cleat	oak	19	25	826	
F	3	shelves	glass	6	82	824	

1 Prepare the side, top and bottom boards, A, B and C, by cutting them to length as detailed. The four boards require a notch that's ¾"-wide by 1¾"-deep. The notches are located 2" from the ends of all pieces. Use a table saw, or handsaw and chisel, to form the notches. Take the time to cut these notches as accurately as possible.

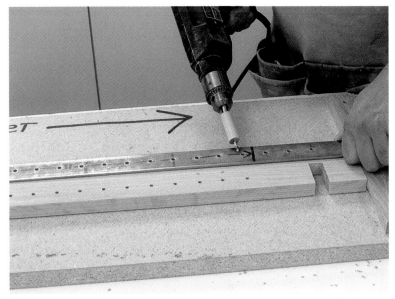

2 Drill two columns of holes in each side board for the adjustable shelf pins. The holes are 1" in from the front and back edges and 1¼" apart. Be sure the boards are oriented properly so the sides are mirror images. Measure and mark the hole positions, or build a simple jig that can be used for many other projects.

3 Use an object about 1½" in diameter and mark an arc on each corner of the top, bottom and side boards.

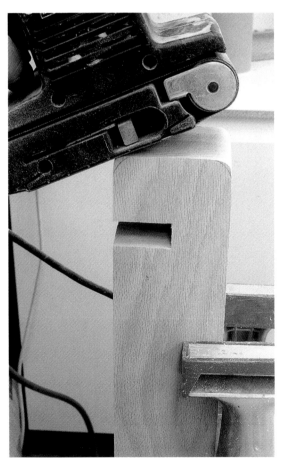

5 Dry fit the parts and mark a line showing the start and finish points that will be used when cutting rabbets on all pieces. The side, top and bottom boards all require a ¼"-wide by ⅜"-deep rabbet, which extends past the marks by ⅜". Cut the rabbets using a router table and straight bit.

4 Use a belt sander to contour the corners by following the marks. Clamp the four boards together and form the corners. This technique ensures that all corners will be identical. Use this "ganged" sanding method when forming the contours on any project where there are a number of identical parts.

6 | Dry fit the parts again and square the corners with a sharp chisel.

7 | Take the shelf frame apart for the last time and finish sand all parts. Apply glue to the notches and clamp the four pieces securely.

8 | The back board D is installed in the rabbets and secured with glue and brad nails. If this board was properly cut with square corners it will align with the shelf frame.

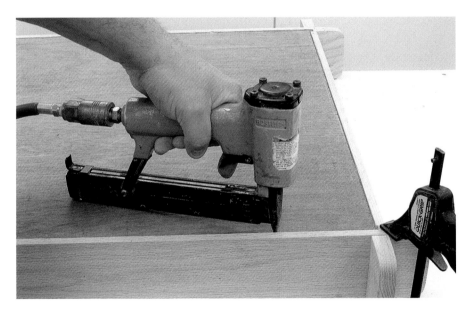

9 | The support cleat E is attached to the back underside of the top board. Use glue and two 1"-long screws in counterbored holes to secure the cleat. Fill the holes with wood plugs.

construction NOTES

This shelf unit can be secured to a wall with two 3" screws drilled through the support cleat and into a stud. Drill counterbored holes and use a wood button to cover the screw heads.

Apply a finish to your shelf unit and order the tempered glass shelves. I will be using three shelves that are $1/4$"-thick by 3"-deep and $32^7/_{16}$"-wide. However, your display may require a different number of shelves. Ask the glass supplier to polish the edges.

If you need a degree of security for your small collectibles, glass doors can be installed. There are a number of door options, the simplest being glass sliders in a track.

Plastic tracks are available at most hardware stores. The upper track is normally higher so the sliding doors can be lifted in and set in the bottom track. These tracks can be surface mounted or installed in routed grooves. Purchase the tracks before ordering the glass to verify the correct thickness.

Swinging glass doors may also be installed. Use hardware that includes hinges and handles, and doesn't require any holes drilled in the glass. It's great hardware and I've used it on many projects.

If you plan on using a wood frame door you can use the shorter version of hidden hinge hardware. The compact series hinges are the perfect hardware solution for wood frame and glass panel doors.

This shelf design can be easily altered to meet any requirements. Build the shelf taller or wider to suit your collectibles. The depth isn't limited to 1×4 stock, so use a wider board if needed. The shelf will be perfect as long as the notch depth is half the board width.

There are many ways to secure the shelf to a wall. If you don't like the cleat method, use a $1/2$"-thick back board. Mounting screws can then be driven at any place on this thicker board. Or simple eyelets can be screwed into the top board and the unit suspended with screws. You may want to inset the back board and install wire hangers to secure the shelf. There are dozens of creative hanging methods, so select one that suits your needs.

Wood screw-hole buttons.

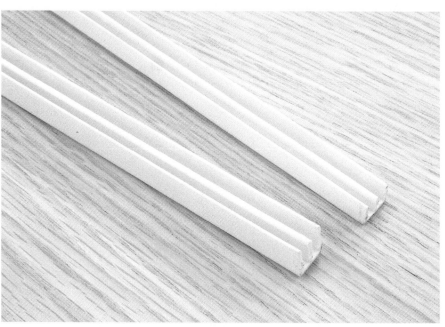

Sliding glass door tracks.

Swinging glass door hardware.

A standard hidden hinge (upper).
Compact series hidden hinges
are the ideal hardware solution
for wood frame glass doors
(lower).

divider-wall display cabinet

My clients wanted this special cabinet to divide a kitchen breakfast area and living room, but they didn't want either area closed off by a solid wall. The solution was this glass-walled cabinet that provides storage and display, yet still maintains that open feeling between the two rooms.

THERE ARE A NUMBER OF structural concerns to consider when building a cabinet of this type. Glass cannot be used as a support panel, so a wood frame is required. Solid wood (in this case I used red oak) is joined to create a skeleton support frame. Even though it's a large, open cabinet, it is extremely sturdy and structurally sound.

The primary joinery method is glue with plate joinery biscuits. This system is a relatively new form of joinery that many experts consider one of the strongest in use today. It's also one of my personal favorites.

As you study the construction procedures you'll notice that I've used a special technique to support the long shelves. Glass shelving is required so the lighting can illuminate the entire cabinet, however, the long lengths of glass caused some concern. I resolved this issue by building a wood and glass hybrid shelf system that proved to be very successful.

My clients wanted a traditional looking cabinet, so I used cathedral doors and crown moulding. The antique handles and Old World-style frame-and-panel construction met the requirements. The cabinet is large, being almost 6' wide and 7' high, but doesn't overpower the rooms.

Mr. and Mrs. McIndoe of Russell, Ontario, own the lovely crystal stemware and figurine collection displayed here.

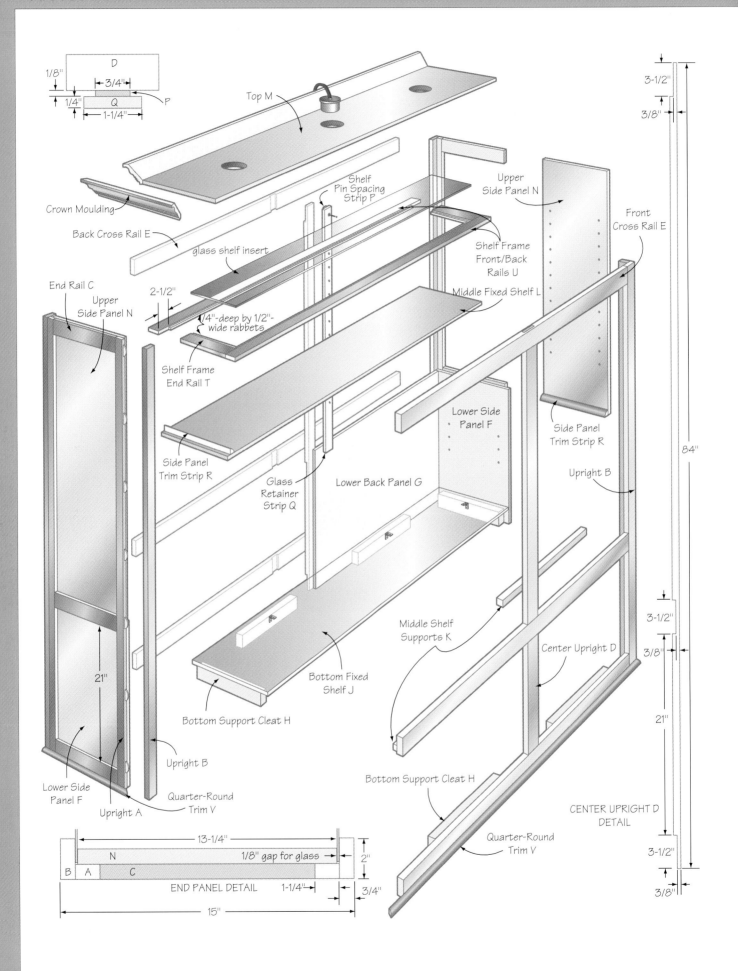

D

1/8"

3/4"

1/4"

1-1/4"

Q

P

Top M

Crown Moulding

Back Cross Rail E

glass shelf insert

End Rail C

Upper
Side Panel N

2-1/2"

1/4"-deep by 1/2"-
wide rabbets

Shelf Frame
End Rail T

Side Panel
Trim Strip R

Glass
Retainer
Strip Q

Lower Back Panel G

Bottom Fixed
Shelf J

Bottom Support Cleat H

Upright A

Upright B

Quarter-Round
Trim V

Lower Side
Panel F

21"

Shelf
Pin Spacing
Strip P

Upper
Side Panel N

Shelf Frame
Front/Back
Rails U

Middle Fixed Shelf L

Lower Side
Panel F

Middle Shelf
Supports K

Front
Cross Rail E

Side Panel
Trim Strip R

Upright B

Center Upright D

Bottom Support Cleat H

Quarter-Round
Trim V

CENTER UPRIGHT D
DETAIL

3-1/2"

3/8"

84"

3-1/2"

3/8"

21"

3-1/2"

3/8"

13-1/4"

N

1/8" gap for glass

2"

B A C

END PANEL DETAIL

1-1/4"

3/4"

15"

42

materials list **inches**

REFERENCE	QUANTITY	PART	STOCK	THICKNESS	WIDTH	LENGTH	COMMENTS
A	4	frame uprights	red oak	$3/4$	$1^1/4$	84	
B	4	frame uprights	red oak	$3/4$	2	84	
C	6	end rails	red oak	$3/4$	$3^1/2$	11	
D	2	center uprights	red oak	$3/4$	2	84	
E	6	front & back cross rails	red oak	$3/4$	$3^1/2$	66	
F	2	lower side panels	oak pb	$11/16$	$13^9/16$	27	
G	2	lower back panels	oak pb	$11/16$	$33^1/2$	27	
H	6	bottom support cleats	softwood	$1^1/2$	$2^3/4$	12	
J	1	bottom fixed shelf	oak pb	$11/16$	$12^7/8$	$67^1/8$	
K	2	middle shelf supports	red oak	$3/4$	$3/4$	20	
L	1	middle fixed shelf	oak pb	$11/16$	$13^9/16$	$68^1/2$	
M	1	top	oak pb	$11/16$	$13^9/16$	$68^1/2$	
N	2	upper side panels	oak pb	$11/16$	$13^1/4$	$55^5/8$	
P	1	shelf pin spacing strip	red oak	$1/8$	$3/4$	$55^5/8$	
Q	1	glass retainer strip	red oak	$1/4$	$1/4$	$55^5/8$	
R	2	side panel trim strips	red oak	$1/2$	$1/2$	$13^3/8$	
S	1	bottom adjustable shelf (not shown in illustration)	oak pb	$11/16$	$12^3/4$	$66^7/8$	
T	6	shelf frame end rails	red oak	$3/4$	$2^1/2$	$9^1/8$	
U	6	shelf frame back & front rails	red oak	$3/4$	$2^1/2$	67	
V	16'	quarter-round trim	red oak	$3/4$	$3/4$		
	1	16' of $4^1/2$" crown moulding					
	4	glass door frames		$3/4$	$16^1/2$	$54^1/2$	
	4	plywood core lower doors		$11/16$	$16^1/2$	23	
	16	107° full-overlay hidden hinges					
	2	back glass panels		$1/8$	$33^5/8$	$53^1/4$	
	4	glass door panels		$1/8$	$12^{11}/16$	$50^{11}/16$	
	3	shelf tempered glass panels		$1/4$	$9^1/16$	$62^{13}/16$	

materials list **millimeters**

REFERENCE	QUANTITY	PART	STOCK	THICKNESS	WIDTH	LENGTH	COMMENTS
A	4	frame uprights	red oak	19	32	2134	
B	4	frame uprights	red oak	19	51	2134	
C	6	end rails	red oak	19	89	279	
D	2	center uprights	red oak	19	51	2134	
E	6	front & back cross rails	red oak	19	89	1676	
F	2	lower side panels	oak pb	18	344	686	
G	2	lower back panels	oak pb	18	851	686	
H	6	bottom support cleats	softwood	38	70	305	
J	1	bottom fixed shelf	oak pb	18	327	1705	
K	2	middle shelf supports	red oak	19	19	508	
L	1	middle fixed shelf	oak pb	18	344	1740	
M	1	top	oak pb	18	344	1740	
N	2	upper side panels	oak pb	18	336	1413	
P	1	shelf pin spacing strip	red oak	3	19	1413	
Q	1	glass retainer strip	red oak	6	32	1413	
R	2	side panel trim strips	red oak	13	13	340	
S	1	bottom adjustable shelf (not shown in illustration)	oak pb	18	324	1698	
T	6	shelf frame end rails	red oak	19	64	1930	
U	6	shelf frame back & front rails	red oak	19	64	1702	
V	5m	quarter-round trim	red oak	19	19		
	1	5m of 115mm crown moulding					
	4	glass door frames		19	419	1385	
	4	plywood core lower doors		18	419	584	
	16	107° full-overlay hidden hinges					
	2	back glass panels		3	854	1352	
	4	glass door panels		3	323	1288	
	3	shelf tempered glass panels		6	231	1596	

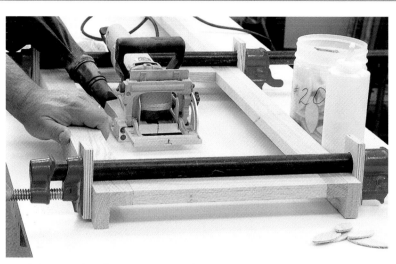

1 | Cut all the frame uprights A and B to size. Join one A upright to one B upright using eight No. 20 biscuits, as shown in the illustration. These four sections are the corner posts for the cabinet, and all faces should be 2" wide.

2 | Join together the corner posts with three end rails C, forming two end frames. Refer to the illustration for rail location. Use No. 20 biscuits to construct the end frames and clamp until the glue has set.

3 | The center uprights and cross rails, D and E, require dado and rabbet cuts before being joined to the end frames. Refer to the illustration for positioning and cut all the joints. Use a table saw, router or a radial arm saw with a dado blade.

4 | Use biscuits to assemble the cabinet frame by joining the two end frames with the six cross rails. Apply glue, join the frames and clamp in place. If you don't have long clamps, use two in tandem as shown in the photograph.

tip

Plate joinery biscuits are very absorbent and will swell in humid areas. You can return them to their original size by drying them in a microwave oven. Use a low setting and monitor their progress to prevent scorching the wood.

5 Fit the center uprights D in place. Secure the joint with glue and clamps, or hold it with a brad nail.

6 Prior to fitting any panels, use a ³⁄₈" roundover bit in a router to dress all but the top and bottom outside edges. Decide on the style of top moulding you plan to use before rounding over the outside corners. Stop the round over far enough below the top, leaving them square. This provides a nice sharp corner for mounting the moulding.

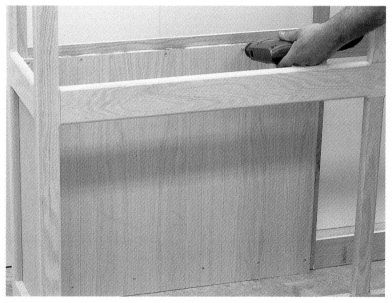

7 Cut the two lower side panels F to size, as detailed in the Materials List. The middle fixed shelf L will sit on top of the panels, ⁵⁄₁₆" below the middle rails. This will allow the two back glass panels to rest on the fixed shelf behind, and below, the middle rail edge. Install the panels flush with the bottom edge of the cabinet frame. Use glue and 1¼" screws to secure the panels. The screws on the back edge, as well as those on the bottom, will be covered with panels. Counterbore screw heads that will be visible and fill with wood plugs.

8 Orient the grain pattern vertically on the back side of the cabinet. I used two back panels G and secured them with glue and screws. Extend a line from the side panel top edges along the back side of the middle rail. Use the line as a guide when installing the back panels to ensure all panels are correctly aligned. Hide any obvious screw heads in counterbored holes filled with wood plugs.

9 | I used scrap softwood from my shop for the six bottom support cleats H. Any wood is suitable because these cleats won't be visible. Attach them with glue and screws ¾" below the top edges of the bottom rails.

10 | The bottom fixed shelf J is attached with glue and ⅝" screws in small, metal, right-angled brackets, from the underside.

11 | The two shelf supports K are secured to the back side of the front middle rail. Use glue and 1¼"-long screws. The top edge of these supports should be 1" below the middle rail's top edge.

12 | Install the top board M with its top surface flush with the frame's top. Use glue and 2" particleboard screws to secure the board. The top crown moulding will hide the screws. Remember to drill pilot holes for the screws to achieve the best connection possible. Note that the cabinet is turned on its side in the photograph to make installation easier. Install the middle fixed shelf L on supports K at this time.

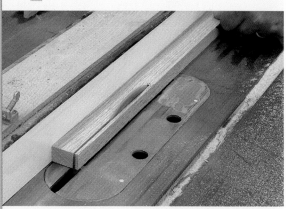

When cutting thin strips of wood on a table saw, keep the widest part of the board between the fence and the blade.

13 | Install 3mm back glass panels, ⅛" thick. Fit the glass between the side panel back edge and frame member. Leave a ¾" space between the panels on the center upright D to provide room for adjustable shelf pin holes. Cut the two side panels N as detailed in the Materials List and secure them in place with glue and 1¼" brads. Be sure to leave that ½" gap at the back edge of the panels for the glass.

14 | Cut the spacing strip P to size. This strip is the same thickness as the back glass panels. It is required so a moulding, which will hold the back glass panels secure, can be installed. Glue and nail this strip in the middle of the center upright.

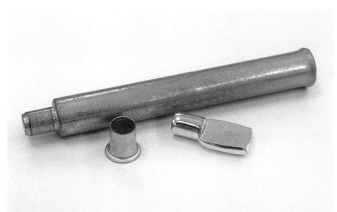

15 | The glass retainer strip Q was sanded and slightly rounded over on each outside face edge. It's secured along the center of the middle upright, on top of the spacing strip, with brass screws. This retainer will hold the two rear glass panels in place and must be removable should the glass need replacing. Shelf pin holes will be drilled through the glass retainer and spacing strips to support the adjustable shelves. I've decided to use a ⅜"-diameter brass pin and sleeve assembly, as it will be very visible.

16 | Make a shelf pin hole jig from a 55"-long hardwood strip. Drill the guide holes 3" apart using a piece of dowel rod on the drill bit to limit the hole depth. Drill two rows of holes on each end panel, as well as on the back face of each center upright.

18 Dress the side to the middle fixed shelf joint by installing ½" quarter-round trim strips R. Apply glue and tack in place with brads. Fill the nail holes with colored putty.

17 After drilling the six columns of holes in the upper section, cut the shelf pin hole jig 23" long. Use the jig as a guide for drilling the adjustable holes in the bottom section. Prepare the bottom adjustable shelf S by cutting it to length and applying iron-on wood veneer edge tape to one long edge. Test fit the shelf.

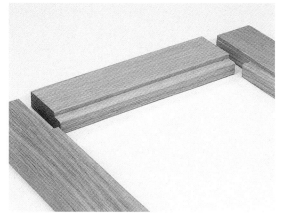

19 Each of the six glass and wood combination shelves in the upper glass section requires a rabbet cut on the inside of the frames. This rabbet will support the glass flush with the top surface of the wood frame. Cut a ¼"-deep by ¼"-wide rabbet on one long edge of each frame member. These rabbets can be cut with a router bit or with a dado blade on your table saw. Notch the rabbets on the front and back rails U as shown in the photo. They are cut back 2½", which will allow the end rails T to align flush with the ends of the back and front rails. Join the rails at each corner with two ⅜"-diameter dowels and glue or with biscuit joinery.

20 Install 4½"-high crown moulding on the left end, back and front of the cabinet. There is no need to install moulding on the right end, as the cabinet will be against a wall. Remember to place the crown moulding upside down on your miter saw. Position it at the same angle as it will rest on the cabinet. In other words, the table on your saw should be thought of as the ceiling and the back guard as the cabinet. If the moulding is oriented properly on your saw you'll get perfect 45° miter cuts every time.

You have the option to build your own doors like the ones detailed in Chapters 7, 8 and 9, or purchase them from a door company as I did.

The sizes are detailed in the Materials List. When determining door width required, add 1" to the interior cabinet width, then divide by two for two doors. This cabinet provides a good example of the definition "cabinet interior width." The smallest width is the cabinet's interior dimension. In this project the width is measured from inside stile-face to inside stile-face, not the cabinet side panels. The stiles in this project are "inside" the cabinet and they determine the cabinet interior width.

I've given the required glass dimensions in the Materials List, but I suggest you wait until you have the doors and complete the cabinet frame before ordering glass. Verify the measurements of your cabinet to be certain of the sizes required. It's very difficult to "trim" a sheet of glass, so it's worth waiting and double-checking the measurements.

21 Each door is installed with two 107° hidden hinges per door. The hinges are attached to face frame mounting plates because the face frame extends into the interior cabinet space.

construction NOTES

I finished my cabinet with one coat of Minwax Provincial Stain and three coats of oil-based polyurethane. Sand between each coat of polyurethane with 220-grit paper.

I doubt that your width and length requirements will be the same as mine. However, these dimensions can be easily changed to suit your needs by altering the cross rail lengths.

You may also need a "left side against the wall" cabinet, so simply change the crown moulding. Both ends are identical and the modifications are simple.

If you want a large display cabinet with its back against a wall just replace the back glass panels with ¼"-thick veneer plywood.

Glass panels that have an etched pattern can add a nice touch to the cabinet, or you might want to add some color by installing colored glass panels for the backs and doors.

This cabinet is versatile and its dimensions are easily changed to suit your requirements. The construction procedures remain the same no matter what size you decide to make your cabinet.

22 Illuminate the cabinet interior with small round lamps that require a hole in the cabinet top board. Lighting kits, consisting of two or three fixtures and a transformer, are available at most home centers. Follow the installation details carefully when installing these lights.

china credenza and hutch

Do you have a storage problem? Are there dozens of dishes and beautiful display pieces stored away in your attic just crying for a perfect display cabinet? If you're like me, there's always a need for more storage. Here's a solution that might just fit the bill.

I BUILT THIS CABINET TO BE installed in an eating area off the kitchen, next to a family room. Since space was an issue in this high traffic area, the cabinet is 12" deep. However, if you're lucky enough to have a lot of space, the base depth can be easily increased. Remember though, if you do build the 12"-deep version, anchor the cabinet to the wall studs.

The lower section of the cabinet is used to store bowls, fondue pots and other specialized cookware. It's accessible so when Aunt Sarah comes to visit you can easily find that strange bowl she gave you as a wedding present. The top section, behind glass doors, features two glass shelves that are ideal for showing off crystal and glassware. And the round side shelves are perfect for displaying collectibles.

I also installed three fluorescent light fixtures; one on top, another in the upper section and the third behind the wide rail above the base top. I located a three-lever switch that fits into a single electrical box and mounted it behind the upper cabinet bottom rail. If the wall unit will be permanently attached you can install wall switches.

The beautiful collection of teapots and glassware shown in this cabinet is owned by Peter and Elaine Marr of Russell, Ontario.

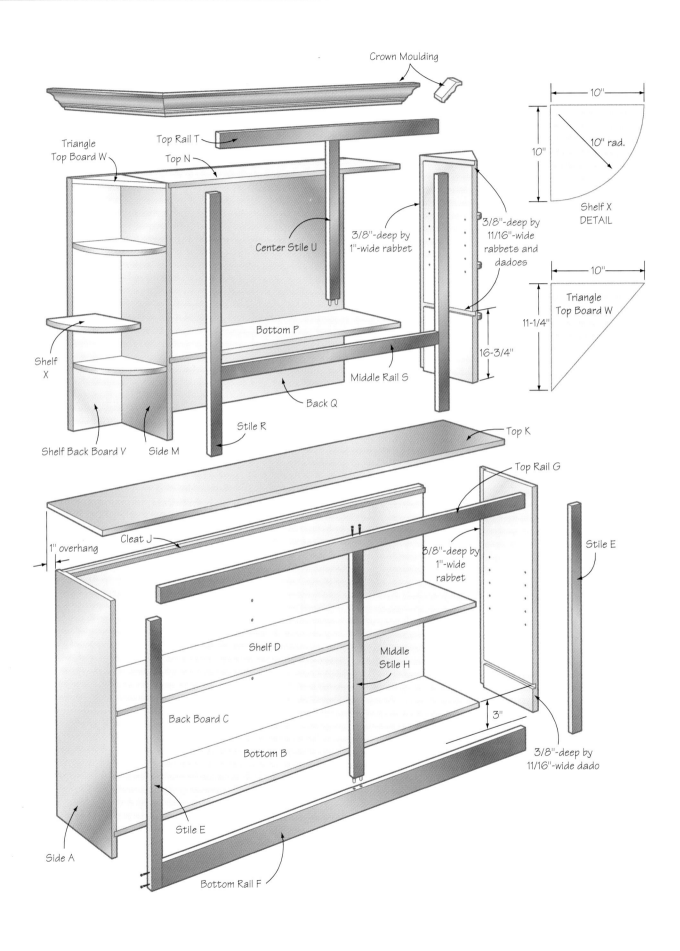

Crown Moulding

Triangle
Top Board W

Top Rail T

Top N

Center Stile U

3/8"-deep by
1"-wide rabbet

3/8"-deep by
11/16"-wide
rabbets and
dadoes

10"

10"

10" rad.

Shelf X
DETAIL

10"

11-1/4"

Triangle
Top Board W

Bottom P

Shelf
X

16-3/4"

Middle Rail S

Back Q

Shelf Back Board V   Side M

Stile R

Top K

Top Rail G

Cleat J

1" overhang

3/8"-deep by
1"-wide
rabbet

Stile E

Shelf D

Middle
Stile H

Back Board C

3"

Bottom B

3/8"-deep by
11/16"-wide dado

Side A

Stile E

Bottom Rail F

materials list | **inches**

REFERENCE	QUANTITY	PART	STOCK	THICKNESS	WIDTH	LENGTH	COMMENTS
A	2	sides	oak pb*	$^{11}/_{16}$	$11^1/_4$	34	
B	1	bottom	oak pb	$^{11}/_{16}$	$10^1/_2$	$71^3/_8$	
C	1	back board	oak pb	$^{11}/_{16}$	34	$71^3/_8$	
D	2	shelves	oak pb	$^{11}/_{16}$	$10^1/_8$	$70^1/_2$	
E	2	stiles	oak	$^3/_4$	$1^1/_2$	34	
F	1	bottom rail	oak	$^3/_4$	3	69	
G	1	top rail	oak	$^3/_4$	$1^1/_2$	69	
H	1	middle stile	oak	$^3/_4$	$1^1/_2$	$29^1/_2$	
J	1	cleat	oak	$^3/_4$	1	$70^3/_8$	
K	1	top	oak	$^3/_4$	13	74	
L	4	doors	oak	$^3/_4$	$17^3/_8$	31	
	8	107° European hidden hinges					

Hutch

REFERENCE	QUANTITY	PART	STOCK	THICKNESS	WIDTH	LENGTH	COMMENTS
M	2	sides	oak pb	$^{11}/_{16}$	$11^1/_4$	46	
N	1	top	oak pb	$^{11}/_{16}$	$10^1/_4$	$51^3/_8$	
P	1	bottom	oak pb	$^{11}/_{16}$	$10^1/_4$	$51^3/_8$	
Q	1	back	oak pb	$^{11}/_{16}$	46	$51^3/_8$	
R	2	stiles	oak	$^3/_4$	$1^1/_2$	46	
S	1	middle rail	oak	$^3/_4$	3	49	
T	1	top rail	oak	$^3/_4$	3	49	
U	1	center stile	oak	$^3/_4$	$1^1/_2$	$26^3/_8$	
V	2	shelf back boards	oak	$^3/_4$	10	46	
W	2	triangle top boards	oak	$^3/_4$	10	$11^1/_8$	
X	6	shelves	oak	$^3/_4$	10	10	A
Y	4	doors	oak	$^3/_4$	$12^3/_8$	$28^1/_2$	
	3	feet of $3^1/_4$ " crown moulding					
	8	107° European hidden hinges					

*particleboard

A: with a radius front

materials list | **millimeters**

REFERENCE	QUANTITY	PART	STOCK	THICKNESS	WIDTH	LENGTH	COMMENTS
A	2	sides	oak pb*	18	285	864	
B	1	bottom	oak pb	18	267	1813	
C	1	back board	oak pb	18	864	1813	
D	2	shelves	oak pb	18	257	1791	
E	2	stiles	oak	19	38	864	
F	1	bottom rail	oak	19	76	1753	
G	1	top rail	oak	19	38	1753	
H	1	middle stile	oak	19	38	750	
J	1	cleat	oak	19	25	1788	
K	1	top	oak	19	330	1880	
L	4	doors	oak	19	442	787	
	8	107° European hidden hinges					

Hutch

REFERENCE	QUANTITY	PART	STOCK	THICKNESS	WIDTH	LENGTH	COMMENTS
M	2	sides	oak pb	18	285	1168	
N	1	top	oak pb	18	260	1305	
P	1	bottom	oak pb	18	260	1305	
Q	1	back	oak pb	18	1168	1305	
R	2	stiles	oak	19	38	1168	
S	1	middle rail	oak	19	76	1245	
T	1	top rail	oak	19	76	1245	
U	1	center stile	oak	19	38	670	
V	2	shelf back boards	oak	19	254	1168	
W	2	triangle top boards	oak	19	254	282	
X	6	shelves	oak	19	254	254	A
Y	4	doors	oak	19	315	724	
	3	2743mm of 82mm crown moulding					
	8	107° European hidden hinges					

*particleboard

A: with a radius front

Building the Credenza

1 Prepare the two side panels A as shown in the Materials List. Cut an $^{11}/_{16}$"-wide by $^3/_8$"-deep dado, 3" up from the bottom edge in each panel. Note that the back board rabbets are cut 1" wide and $^3/_8$" deep to accept an $^{11}/_{16}$"-thick back board. As you know, most walls aren't straight so it's difficult to tightly fit a wide, flat back board. The extended side panels usually make it easier to get a tight fit.

2 Cut and install the bottom board B. Secure it in the dadoes with glue, and clamp tightly or nail from the outside of the side panels. Use two $2^1/_2$" finishing nails per side; sink the nail heads and fill the holes with colored putty.

3 Place the back board C in the side rabbets and secure using glue and $2^1/_2$" finishing nails from the back. The thick back board serves three purposes. First, it adds weight to the shallow base. Secondly, it supports the bottom fixed shelf using glue and 2" screws 6" apart through the back board. And third, the board is thick enough to accept holes for the adjustable shelf pins which will provide the necessary support for the long shelves.

tip

It's common to tear the veneer when cross-grain cutting with a dado blade in your table saw. To prevent this, cut through the veneer with a sharp knife before using the table saw. A router gives the cleanest cut, but use carbide-tipped bits because of the high glue content in particleboard.

4 Install the two outside stiles E using glue and face nail with 2½" finishing nails. Fill the nail holes with colored putty. The stiles are attached flush with the outside edges of the credenza sides. If you prefer, the stiles can be attached with glue and biscuits.

6 The middle stile H is attached to the bottom rail with glue and two ⅜" dowels. The top end is secured with 2" wood screws through the top edge of the top rail. Install the stile so there is equal spacing on both sides.

5 The bottom rail F is glued and nailed flush with the top surface of the bottom board. Drill and counterbore two holes in the edge of each stile. Secure the stiles to the bottom rail with glue and 2" wood screws. The counterbored holes are filled with ⅜" wood plugs. The top rail G is also secured with glue and two 2" screws through the stiles, then the holes are filled with wood plugs. Its top edge is flush with the stiles' top ends. This rail will be strengthened when it's screwed into the credenza top board.

construction NOTES

For this project I purchased ready-made cathedral oak doors. I used standard 107° full-overlay European hidden hinges with face-frame-style mounting plates. Drill the 35mm holes in the doors and install the hinges as detailed by the manufacturer.

There are many options when doors are being considered. The simplest method, which doesn't involve any tools, is to purchase doors from a supplier. They are reasonably priced, and there are dozens of door factories looking for your business.

You can use the door-building techniques in Chapters 7, 8, and 9, or if you want to explore the whole range of door options take a look at my book, *Building Cabinet Doors and Drawers*.

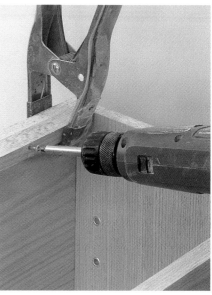

7 Drill holes for the adjustable shelf pins. I used ⅜"-diameter brass shelf pins, spaced 2" apart. There are two columns of holes in each side panel, one column in the middle of the back board and another on the inside face of the middle stile. Use a piece of scrap wood to make a jig for the shelf holes. Cut the two shelves D for the base section, then apply wood veneer tape to the front edge of each shelf. Now is an ideal time to fill any nail holes, sand the cabinet and round over the outside edges of the stiles with a ⅜" router bit.

8 Cut and secure the wood cleat J flush with the top inside edge of the back board. Use glue and 1¼" screws to fasten the cleat.

9 Glue up ¾"-thick boards to form a top K that's 13" deep and 74" wide. Glue-ups are best accomplished using biscuit joinery, although a simple edge glue joint will be fine for this application. Slightly ease the two front corners of the top with a belt sander to eliminate the sharp corners. Round over the top and bottom, front and side edges with a ⅜" roundover bit in a router. Drill pilot holes in the cleat J and top rail G for screws that will secure the top. Attach the top using 2" wood screws, making sure there is a 1" overhang on the front edge and at each end. The screws are installed from the underside of the cleat and top rail into the top. I spaced my screws 12" apart. Don't use any glue, and run the drill bit from side to side in the cleat and top rail to make the screw holes larger. This will let the solid wood top move when it expands and contracts with humidity changes.

Building the Hutch

10 Cut the two upper side panels M as shown in the Materials List, then cut the ³/₈"-deep dadoes and rabbets as detailed in the illustration. Note that the rabbet for the back board is cut 1" wide to accept an ¹¹/₁₆"-thick panel. This leaves enough room to route the lighting wires behind the back board. The top N and bottom P can be glued and clamped into the dadoes and rabbets. The top board can be nailed from the outside edge of the side because a board will be installed over the nail heads.

11 Secure the back board Q to the cabinet, in the rabbets, with glue and finishing nails. Drive the nails through the back board into the cabinet sides at a slight angle and set the nail heads. The back board is attached flush with the top edge of the cabinet side boards.

12 Glue and face nail the two outside stiles R flush with the outside face of the cabinet side boards. Again, use biscuits to attach the stiles if you prefer. Cut the middle rail S to length and attach it to the bottom P. It is secured with glue and face nailed flush with the top surface of the shelf. Install 2" wood screws in counterbored holes through the outside edge of the stiles into the middle rail. Fill the holes with wood plugs and sand flush. Cut the top rail T and clamp it in place. Do not secure it at this time because you want to mark the center stile to install dowels in the top and bottom rails.

13 Align the center stile U with equal spacing on both sides and mark the dowel positions. After drilling, insert the dowels and clamp the center stile in place. Glue and face nail the top rail flush with the top surface of the top board. Again, use 2" screws in counterbored holes through the outside edge of the stiles into the top rail. Fill the holes with wood plugs. Fill all the nail holes with colored putty to match your finish. With a ⅜" roundover bit, round over the outside edges of the outer stiles, the lower edge of the middle rail and inside edges of the outside stiles in the lower opening. Be sure to stop rounding over the edges of the outer stiles ¾" from the top so the crown moulding fits tightly to the cabinet. Drill the adjustable shelf pin holes in the same manner as the credenza.

15 Prepare two triangle top boards W, as shown in the illustration. Attach each one flush with the top surface of the upper section using glue and 1½" wood screws. Install the screws through the front edge of the triangle boards; the crown moulding will cover that edge.

14 Cut the two solid oak shelf back boards V as detailed in the Materials List. Attach each one flush with the back edge of the side boards using glue and 1½" wood screws.

16 Cut the six shelves X as shown in the illustration. Use a compass to draw the arc and cut with a jigsaw. Clamp all six shelves together and sand all of them as one unit to ensure they are identical. Sand the shelves, then round over the top and bottom edges of the radius curve with a ⅜" roundover bit. Attach the shelves with glue and screws. Position the shelves to suit your needs, but try and align them with the ⅜"-diameter shelf pin holes. If that position is suitable, screws can be inserted through the shelf pin holes into the shelf boards. If the pin holes don't align with the shelves, use two screws through the back board V into the shelf, and one directly behind the upper stile. Fill the counterbored holes with wood plugs.

17 Any style of top moulding can be applied. I used 3¼" crown moulding. Some of the angles are tricky, but remember, when cutting angles in crown moulding you should place it upside down in the miter box. The front angle on my cabinet was 41°, but yours may be slightly different. I cut each moulding at 20.5° to equal the 41° corner. There are also two little pieces of moulding that are required on each end, and the angle can be a test of your cutting skills. To make matters more complicated, the moulding is only ¾"-long at the bottom. Take your time and make a couple of test cuts. All that's required is patience to get a nice tight fit.

construction NOTES

I ordered two ¼"-thick by 10⅛"-deep by 50⅜"-long tempered glass shelves for the upper section of the cabinet. Verify the measurements on your cabinet before ordering the glass.

You'll need four doors 12⅜"-wide by 28½"-high that are designed to accept glass center panels. They are installed with European hidden hinges. For the upper section doors, I used Blum Compact 33 style face frame hinges because of the small stile mounting plate. However, any European-style hinge will work with these doors, and many of the traditional-style hinges will work equally well.

I finished my cabinet with three coats of oil-based polyurethane. I cut the first coat with thinner by 10% and sanded with 220-grit paper between each coat.

The final color, your décor and the type of wood used will determine your finish. However, this cabinet will look great in whatever wood or color you decide to use.

Installing lights is optional. I'm a bit of a gadget nut so I installed one 36" fluorescent lamp on top of the cabinet, one behind the hutch top rail and another behind the hutch middle rail.

I found a unique three-lever switch at my local home improvement center that I installed in a single surface-mounted electrical box. I installed the box behind the middle rail where it cannot be seen. I routed the wires behind the back board to an octagon junction box on top of the cabinet. Then I had an electrician connect a supply wire from the service panel to power the lights. While the electrician was there, I had him check my cabinet wiring.

There's not too much involved when installing this cabinet. I suggest you secure the top section to the base with screws through the underside of the credenza top and into the upper cabinet sides. Also, as mentioned previously, the cabinet is tall and shallow so I strongly suggest you attach it to the wall studs with a few 3" screws, just to be safe.

contemporary display and storage cabinet

The style of this project is sleek and modern with very clean lines. It is a contemporary piece with lots of display area and valuable storage space.

CONTEMPORARY FURNITURE is most often flat paneled without the detailed mouldings common to more traditional cabinets. Adding accent strips or color differences creates visual interest. I decided to add two bands of dark walnut as a sharp contrast to the natural finished oak. The hardware also has clean, simple lines, which are a common design treatment of modern-styled furniture.

Three glass shelves provide a surprising amount of display space. These shelves are 12½" deep, so there's room for large collectibles. The greater depth also increases the cabinet's stability. However, the depth is a design choice and can be altered to suit your

collection. Build it at least 12" deep if you want a freestanding unit, and less than 12" if you plan on anchoring the cabinet to a wall. With all its glass, it would be very dangerous to have this cabinet topple. If you have any concern about its stability, please anchor the cabinet to a wall stud.

The impressive collection of antique photographic equipment shown here is a dramatic contrast to the modern styling of this cabinet and makes for a visual treat.

Michael Bowie of Lux Photography in Ottawa, Ontario, owns the camera collection. Michael is responsible for the lead project photos, and is also the technical expert for the step-by-step photography in all of my books.

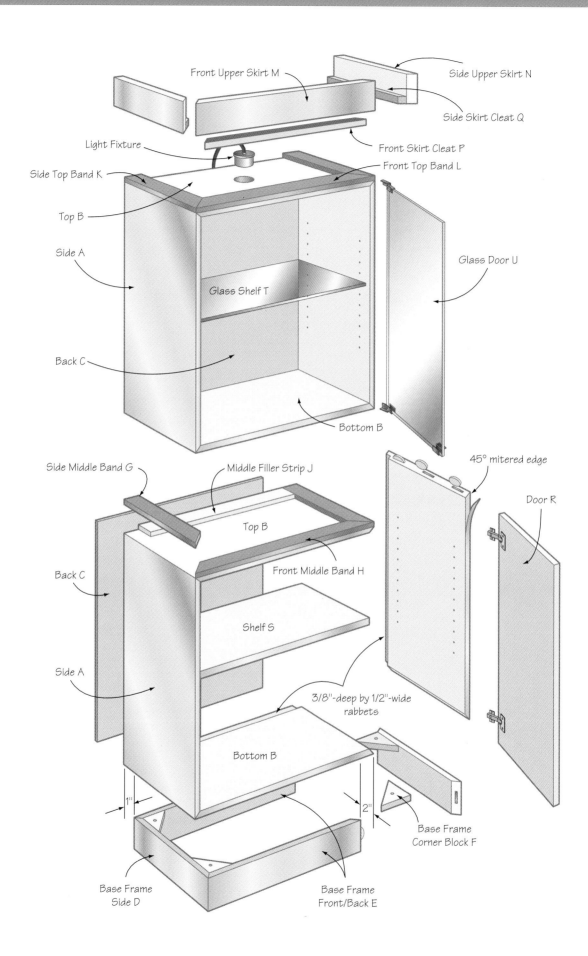

Front Upper Skirt M

Side Upper Skirt N

Side Skirt Cleat Q

Light Fixture

Front Skirt Cleat P

Side Top Band K

Front Top Band L

Top B

Side A

Glass Door U

Glass Shelf T

Back C

Bottom B

Side Middle Band G

Middle Filler Strip J

45° mitered edge

Top B

Door R

Back C

Front Middle Band H

Shelf S

Side A

3/8"-deep by 1/2"-wide rabbets

Bottom B

1"

2"

Base Frame Corner Block F

Base Frame Side D

Base Frame Front/Back E

materials list | **inches**

REFERENCE	QUANTITY	PART	STOCK	THICKNESS	WIDTH	LENGTH	COMMENTS
A	4	sides	oak particleboard	$3/4$	14	35	ends angled at 45°
B	4	tops & bottoms	oak particleboard	$3/4$	14	42	ends angled at 45°
C	2	backs	oak particleboard	$1/2$	$34^1/4$	$41^1/4$	
D	2	base frame sides	oak particleboard	$3/4$	3	12	ends angled at 45°
E	2	base frame fronts & backs	oak particleboard	$3/4$	3	38	ends angled at 45°
F	4	base frame corner blocks	oak particleboard	$3/4$	3	3	cut as a right-angled triangle
G	2	side middle bands	oak particleboard	$3/4$	$1^1/2$	14	with a 45° angle cut on the fronts
H	1	front middle band	oak particleboard	$3/4$	$1^1/2$	42	ends angled at 45°
J	1	middle filler strip	oak particleboard	$3/4$	$2^1/2$	39	
K	2	side top bands	oak particleboard	$3/4$	$1^1/2$	14	with a 45° angle cut on the fronts
L	1	front top band	oak particleboard	$3/4$	$1^1/2$	42	ends angled at 45°
M	1	front upper skirt	oak particleboard	$3/4$	$3^1/4$	42	ends angled at 45°
N	2	side upper skirts	oak particleboard	$3/4$	$3^1/4$	14	with a 45° angle cut on the fronts
P	1	front skirt cleat	oak particleboard	$3/4$	$3/4$	42	ends angled at 45°
Q	2	side skirt cleats	oak particleboard	$3/4$	$3/4$	14	with a 45° angle cut on the fronts
R	2	doors	oak particleboard	$3/4$	$34^3/4$	$20^3/4$	all edges covered in iron-on veneer/full overlay
S	2	lower shelves	oak particleboard	$3/4$	13	$40^3/8$	
T	3	shelves	glass	$1/4$	$12^1/2$	$40^1/2$	tempered
U	2	doors	glass	$1/4$	33	$20^3/16$	

materials list | **millimeters**

REFERENCE	QUANTITY	PART	STOCK	THICKNESS	WIDTH	LENGTH	COMMENTS
A	4	sides	oak particleboard	19	356	889	ends angled at 45°
B	4	tops & bottoms	oak particleboard	19	356	1067	ends angled at 45°
C	2	backs	oak particleboard	13	870	1047	
D	2	base frame sides	oak particleboard	19	76	305	ends angled at 45°
E	2	base frame fronts & backs	oak particleboard	19	76	965	ends angled at 45°
F	4	base frame corner blocks	oak particleboard	19	76	76	cut as a right-angled triangle
G	2	side middle bands	oak particleboard	19	38	356	with a 45° angle cut on the fronts
H	1	front middle band	oak particleboard	19	38	1067	ends angled at 45°
J	1	middle filler strip	oak particleboard	19	64	991	
K	2	side top bands	oak particleboard	19	38	356	with a 45° angle cut on the fronts
L	1	front top band	oak particleboard	19	38	1067	ends angled at 45°
M	1	front upper skirt	oak particleboard	19	82	1067	ends angled at 45°
N	2	side upper skirts	oak particleboard	19	82	356	with a 45° angle cut on the fronts
P	1	front skirt cleat	oak particleboard	19	19	1067	ends angled at 45°
Q	2	side skirt cleats	oak particleboard	19	19	356	with a 45° angle cut on the fronts
R	2	doors	oak particleboard	19	883	527	all edges covered in iron-on veneer/full overlay
S	2	lower shelves	oak particleboard	19	330	1026	
T	3	shelves	glass	6	318	1029	tempered
U	2	doors	glass	6	838	513	

construction NOTES

Before you begin cutting the sides, tops and bottoms to length, consider this option if you don't want the mitered corners. This alternative case construction method using butt joinery is easier than the mitered-corner system. The butt joinery system uses biscuits or screws and glue. The tops and bottoms sit on the side boards and the exposed edges are covered with heat-activated preglued veneer tape. Many woodworkers find this alternative method easier and just as strong. The only change between this and the corner miter joint is the back board rabbet. It must be stopped ¼" short of the ends on the top and bottom boards. Either method is acceptable — the choice is yours. I will detail the corner-miter method in the step-by-step photos in this chapter. The dimensions given in the Materials List are based on the mitered corner, so change them accordingly if you prefer the butt joinery system.

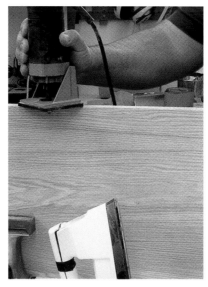

1 Rip four lengths of ¾"-thick veneer plywood from two sheets. Each panel will be 14" wide and 96" long. These four panels will be used for the sides, tops and bottom boards, A and B. The panels will be cut to length with 45° miters on both ends. However, one front edge of each panel must have veneer edge tape applied before cutting the miters on a table saw. This will give you well defined angle cuts on the edge tape. Use ⅞"-wide, preglued, heat-activated veneer edge tape that's applied with an iron. Remove the excess wood tape with a trim bit in your router.

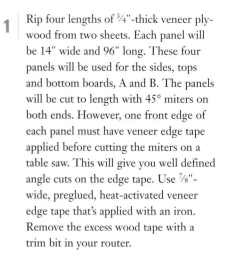

2 Miter cut the eight panels — four sides, two tops and two bottoms, at 45° — to the sizes detailed in the Materials List. The sizes stated are at the longest point of the miter cut. The cutting is easily accomplished on a table saw.

3 Build a simple jig, such as the one shown, to drill two columns of holes in each side panel. These will be used for the adjustable shelf pins and should be the proper diameter for the pins you plan to use. These holes are 3⁄16"-diameter for the brass pins I've chosen. Two mirror-imaged sets of holes are drilled on the inside face of each panel.

4 Each side, top and bottom panel requires a ⅜"-deep by ½"-wide rabbet to receive the back panel. All cuts are located on the rear inside faces of the panels. Make the rabbet cuts with a table saw, router or router table and straight bit.

5 Use No. 0 biscuits and glue to join the four mitered corners on the upper and lower case. Cut the biscuit slots, being careful not to puncture the outside face of the panel. Clamp each carcass until the adhesive sets.

6 Install the backs C on each carcass, in the rabbets, securing them with glue and nails. Verify the exact measurements before cutting these back boards. Remember, if the back boards are cut square, the cabinet carcass will be square.

7 The base frame is made with ¾"-thick veneer plywood. Miter the ends of the four boards D and E at 45°. Reinforce the corner joints with biscuits and apply glue before clamping the frame. Install the four angled corner blocks F with glue and nails. They will strengthen the base frame, square the corners and will be used to attach the frame to the lower carcass.

8 Attach the base frame to the lower cabinet carcass by drilling a hole through each corner block. Use glue and one 1¼"-long screw through each block into the underside of the cabinet carcass. Align the frame so it's 2" back from the front edge and 1" in on each side of the cabinet.

9 The middle banding, G and H, is a darker wood than the cabinet carcass in order to create visual interest. I used walnut to contrast with the lighter oak of the cases. The front band requires a 45° miter on each end. Both sides are cut with the same miter on the front end only. The filler strip J is a piece of any ¾"-thick material in your shop and is installed to support the back edge of the upper carcass. Attach all the strips flush with the outside faces of the carcass using glue and 1¼"-long screws.

10 Drill a series of ¼"-diameter holes, spaced 6" apart, around the perimeter of the banding and filler strip boards. The holes are drilled through the banding and lower carcass top board. They will be used as locator holes when joining the upper with the lower carcass.

12 Lay the cabinet on its back. Cut and install the top banding K and L following the same procedures as the lower banding. Use glue and 1¼"-long screws to attach the three boards.

11 Apply glue on the banding and filler strip boards. Install the top section flush with the banding face edges. Use 2"-long screws in the previously drilled pilot holes to secure the sections.

13 The upper skirt is mainly decorative but serves as a guard to hide the cabinet lamp. The front and side skirts M and N are installed flush with the banding face edges. The corners of the skirt boards are mitered at 45° and ¾"-square cleats P and Q are attached to the skirt boards. These cleats will be used to secure the skirt assembly. Rough cut the three skirt boards a little longer than required, and attach the cleats flush with the lower edges on the back face. Now, miter cut the skirt boards to the lengths given in the Materials List. This procedure will miter both skirt and cleat boards in one operation.

14 Drive 2"-long screws through pilot holes in the cleats to secure the skirt flush with the top banding boards. Use glue on all the joints, including the skirt board corners. Reinforce the skirt corners with a right-angle metal bracket and ⅝"-long screws.

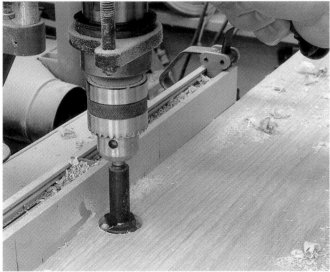

15 Two styles of lower doors R can be installed using full-overlay hidden hinges. The first is an inset door set flush with the cabinet edges, and the second is a full-overlay door that covers the cabinet's front edges. I will be using full-overlay doors but either style is suitable. If you decide to use the inset door style, be sure the cabinet is square. Inset doors reveal a ¹⁄₁₆" gap around the edge, and you will need two doors at 33⅜"-high by 20⅛"-wide. The overlay door width, using full-overlay hidden hinges, is determined by adding 1" to the inside cabinet dimension and dividing by two. For this project, the interior width is 40½"; add 1" and the total is 41½". Dividing that dimension by two means that we need two 20¾" doors for this cabinet. Cut the doors to size, apply heat activated iron-on veneer edge tape to the four edges of each door and drill two 35mm holes per door. The holes are ⅛" from the edge. Space the hinge holes 4" from the top and bottom of each door.

16 To mount the doors, install the 107° hinges with their mounting plates on each door. Hold the door in its open position with a ⅛"-thick spacer between the door edge and cabinet front edge. In this case I've aligned the bottom of the doors flush with the lower edge of the cabinet's bottom board. Drive ⅝"-long screws through the hinge plate holes into the cabinet side board to secure the door. Follow the same procedure for the second door and align if necessary.

17 Cut the two lower shelves S, apply edge tape to the front edge and test fit.

18 Install the tempered glass shelves T. I will be using three shelves that are $\frac{1}{4}$"-thick with polished edges. My shelf pins are $\frac{3}{16}$"-diameter solid brass.

tip

After verifying your measurements, it is an ideal time to order the tempered glass shelves and door, T and U. It's also the perfect time to apply a finish to the cabinet before installing any hardware.

I've used three coats of Fabulon semigloss polyurethane and sanded with 320-grit sandpaper between each coat. The final finish treatment is a coat of clear paste, applied with #0000 steel wool for added protection.

19 The glass door hinges used here are a simple swing model on a pivot pin, commonly found in hardware or glass supply stores. The hinges are mounted as an inset style and the glass doesn't require any drilled holes. Mount the hinge hardware before ordering the glass, thereby allowing yourself to verify the measurements. Dimensions differ slightly from one hardware manufacturer to the next, so it pays to double-check the dimensions.

construction
NOTES

The tempered glass shelves are strong and able to support most collectibles. However, if the items are heavy it would be wise to drill a row of support holes for pins in the cabinet back board.

If the items you plan to display are extremely heavy, a wood back or brace can be installed on the rear edge of each shelf. Cut a groove in one edge of a 1×2 board, about ¾" deep, and slip it over the glass shelf. Use adhesive silicon to secure this strong back.

Any dimension of this cabinet can be altered to suit your requirements, and different wood accent strips can be used to match the existing furniture in the room where this cabinet will be used.

If you are comfortable with wood inlay techniques, interesting designs can be used on the lower wood doors. Design possibilities are endless and limited only by your imagination.

20 My lamp assembly is black to match the hinge hardware. Installing the light is optional, but if you do decide to put lights in your cabinet, purchase the unit and follow the manufacturer's instructions.

21 My glass door hinges and lamp assembly are black so I decided to install black door handles. The lower door handles are plain in keeping with the contemporary style of this cabinet. The glass door handles are a metal slip-on type, readily available at hardware stores. The doors are held closed with a magnetic catch.

corner china and display cabinet

A corner china and display cabinet is one of the most popular woodworking projects — if not *the* most popular. When you talk about cabinets someone is sure to mention their desire for a corner cabinet. If you make one and show it to family and friends, be prepared to make a few more!

I'VE APPLIED MOULDING TO the top and bottom of this cabinet to match existing furniture. It is a simple, rounded-over trim with very little detail. However, you can dramatically change the looks by installing crown or any of the more intricate mouldings available. The basic design can be transformed into any period-style furniture with the appropriate base and top moulding.

I know that this cabinet project seems to be complicated at first glance, and some woodworkers are intimidated by its apparent complexity, but in reality this corner cabinet is easy to build.

I used ¾"-thick veneer plywood for the carcass construction. It's a strong and stable product, and the perfect choice for this corner cabinet. The only solid wood pieces are the trim and door components.

This cabinet features inset cope-and-stick doors. They are made using a rail-and-stile router bit set,

as well as a panel-raising bit. These bits are expensive, but if you plan to make a number of doors they are worth the investment. Remember, take your time making these doors and verify all measurements. They will be installed with only a small gap between the face frame and door, so any error will be obvious.

Jeanne and Jack Chaters of Prescott, Ontario, own the beautiful collection of pottery and specialty dishes displayed here.

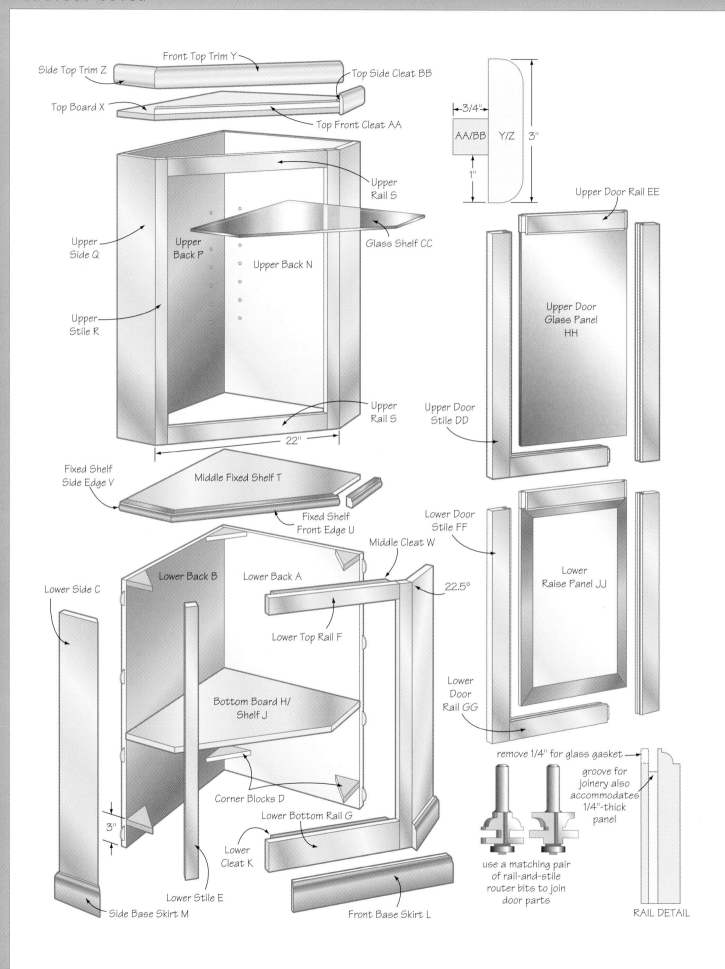

Side Top Trim Z

Front Top Trim Y

Top Side Cleat BB

Top Board X

Top Front Cleat AA

3/4"

AA/BB   Y/Z   3"

1"

Upper Door Rail EE

Upper Rail S

Upper Side Q

Upper Back P

Glass Shelf CC

Upper Back N

Upper Door Glass Panel HH

Upper Stile R

Upper Door Stile DD

Upper Rail S

22"

Fixed Shelf Side Edge V

Middle Fixed Shelf T

Lower Door Stile FF

Fixed Shelf Front Edge U

Middle Cleat W

Lower Raise Panel JJ

Lower Back B

Lower Back A

Lower Side C

Lower Top Rail F

22.5°

Bottom Board H/ Shelf J

Lower Door Rail GG

remove 1/4" for glass gasket

groove for joinery also accommodates 1/4"-thick panel

Corner Blocks D

Lower Bottom Rail G

3"

Lower Cleat K

Lower Stile E

use a matching pair of rail-and-stile router bits to join door parts

Side Base Skirt M

Front Base Skirt L

RAIL DETAIL

materials list | **inches**

REFERENCE	QUANTITY	PART	STOCK	THICKNESS	WIDTH	LENGTH	COMMENTS
A	1	lower back	oak plywood	$3/4$	$22^3/4$	36	
B	1	lower back	oak plywood	$3/4$	22	36	
C	2	lower sides	oak plywood	$3/4$	8	36	angle cut at 22.5°
D	6	corner blocks	oak	$3/4$	3	3	right-angle triangle
E	2	lower stiles	oak	$3/4$	$1^1/2$	36	angle cut at 22.5 °
F	1	lower top rail	oak	$3/4$	2	19	
G	1	lower bottom rail	oak	$3/4$	4	19	
H	1	bottom board	oak plywood	$3/4$	24	24	cut as detailed
J	1	shelf	oak plywood	$3/4$	24	24	cut as detailed
K	1	lower cleat	oak	$3/4$	$3/4$	19	
L	1	front base skirt	oak	$3/4$	3	$22^5/8$	angle cut
M	2	side base skirts	oak	$3/4$	3	$8^1/4$	angle cut
N	1	upper back	oak plywood	$3/4$	$22^3/4$	36	
P	1	upper back	oak plywood	$3/4$	22	36	
Q	2	upper sides	oak plywood	$3/4$	8	36	angle cut at 22.5 °
R	2	upper stiles	oak	$3/4$	$1^1/2$	36	angle cut at 22.5 °
S	2	upper rails	oak	$3/4$	$1^1/2$	19	
T	1	middle fixed shelf	oak plywood	$3/4$	24	24	cut as detailed
U	1	fixed shelf front edge	oak	$3/4$	$1^1/4$	$23^3/4$	angle cut
V	2	fixed shelf side edges	oak	$3/4$	$1^1/4$	$8^1/2$	angle cut
W	1	middle cleat	oak	$3/4$	$3/4$	19	
X	1	top board	oak plywood	$3/4$	24	24	cut as detailed
Y	1	front top trim	oak	$3/4$	3	$22^1/2$	angle cut
Z	2	side top trim	oak	$3/4$	3	$8^3/8$	angle cut
AA	1	top front cleat	oak	$3/4$	$3/4$	$22^1/2$	angle cut
BB	2	top side cleats	oak	$3/4$	$3/4$	$8^3/8$	angle cut
CC	2	shelves	glass	$1/4$	24	24	cut as detailed // use tempered glass
DD	2	upper door stiles	oak	$3/4$	$2^1/4$	33	
EE	2	upper door rails	oak	$3/4$	$2^1/4$	$15^1/2$	dimensions based on cutter set used
FF	2	lower door stiles	oak	$3/4$	$2^1/4$	30	
GG	2	lower door rails	oak	$3/4$	$2^1/4$	$15^1/2$	dimensions based on cutter set used
HH	1	upper door	glass panel	$1/8$	$15^1/16$	$29^1/16$	dimensions based on cutter set used
JJ	1	lower raised panel	oak	$5/8$ -$3/4$	$15^1/4$	$26^1/4$	see step #22 for panel thickness details

materials list | **millimeters**

REFERENCE	QUANTITY	PART	STOCK	THICKNESS	WIDTH	LENGTH	COMMENTS
A	1	lower back	oak plywood	19	578	914	
B	1	lower back	oak plywood	19	559	914	
C	2	lower sides	oak plywood	19	203	914	angle cut at 22.5°
D	6	corner blocks	oak	19	76	76	right-angle triangle
E	2	lower stiles	oak	19	38	914	angle cut at 22.5°
F	1	lower top rail	oak	19	51	483	
G	1	lower bottom rail	oak	19	102	483	
H	1	bottom board	oak plywood	19	610	610	cut as detailed
J	1	shelf	oak plywood	19	610	610	cut as detailed
K	1	lower cleat	oak	19	19	483	
L	1	front base skirt	oak	19	76	575	angle cut
M	2	side base skirts	oak	19	76	209	angle cut
N	1	upper back	oak plywood	19	578	914	
P	1	upper back	oak plywood	19	559	914	
Q	2	upper sides	oak plywood	19	203	914	angle cut at 22.5°
R	2	upper stiles	oak	19	38	914	angle cut at 22.5°
S	2	upper rails	oak	19	38	483	
T	1	middle fixed shelf	oak plywood	19	610	610	cut as detailed
U	1	fixed shelf front edge	oak	19	32	603	angle cut
V	2	fixed shelf side edges	oak	19	32	216	angle cut
W	1	middle cleat	oak	19	19	483	
X	1	top board	oak plywood	19	610	610	cut as detailed
Y	1	front top trim	oak	19	76	572	angle cut
Z	2	side top trim	oak	19	76	213	angle cut
AA	1	top front cleat	oak	19	19	572	angle cut
BB	2	top side cleats	oak	19	19	213	angle cut
CC	2	shelves	glass	6	610	610	cut as detailed // use tempered glass
DD	2	upper door stiles	oak	19	57	838	
EE	2	upper door rails	oak	19	57	394	dimensions based on cutter set used
FF	2	lower door stiles	oak	19	57	762	
GG	2	lower door rails	oak	19	57	394	dimensions based on cutter set used
HH	1	upper door	glass panel	3	383	739	dimensions based on cutter set used
JJ	1	lower raised panel	oak	16-19	387	666	see step #22 for panel thickness details

If you are having difficulty achieving a tight joint between the face frame stiles and side boards, increase the stile angle to 23°. This ensures that the stile front edge contacting the angled edge of the side board will be the first point of contact between the two boards. This is a technique often used by trim carpenters to ensure a tight joint where it's most visible.

1 Cut the two lower back panels A and B to size as detailed in the Materials List. Join them with biscuits or 2" screws and glue. Each back should measure 22" on the inside face. Notice that back A is ¾" wider than B to account for the overlap joint.

2 The lower side panels C are ¾"-thick plywood veneer with a 22.5° angle on one long edge. Join them to the back panels with biscuits and glue.

3 The six corner blocks D are installed with glue and screws in pilot holes. The three upper blocks are attached flush with the upper edges of the side and back panels. The lower blocks are secured with their top faces 3" above the bottom edges of the cabinet. These support blocks are right-angle triangles cut from 1×4 stock.

4 Cut the two stiles and two rails E, F and G for the lower face frame using ¾"-thick solid wood. Each stile has a 22.5° outside edge to match the cuts on the side panels. Notice that the bottom rail is 4" high and the top is 2" high. Join the stiles to both rails using glue and screws in counterbored holes, making certain the screw heads are below the surface. Two 2" screws and glue per joint will secure the face frame.

6 Create a template for the base bottom board and shelf, H and J. Trace around the perimeter of the base and carefully cut the template. Trace the pattern on a piece of ¾"-thick veneer plywood and cut ¾" inside all the lines for the bottom fixed board. Use the pattern once again and cut ¹³⁄₁₆" inside the perimeter of the trace lines for the adjustable lower shelf. Attach the lower cleat K to the inside face of the lower rail. It will be aligned so its top surface is 3" above the bottom edge. Set the bottom board on the corner blocks and cleat. Secure this board with 1¼" screws and glue, in piloted holes, through the cleats and corner blocks.

5 Join the face frame to the cabinet carcass using biscuits and glue. Clamp the joint tightly until the glue sets.

tip

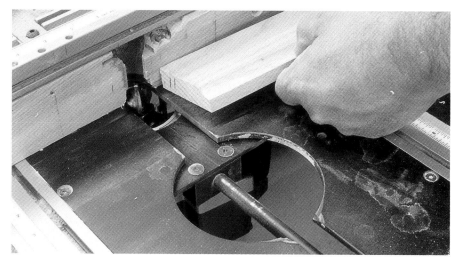

7 My base skirt is 3" high with a decorative edge on the top. For this project I used a cove bit in my router table to complete the cuts. However, any decorative trim bit can be used.

8 Install the base skirt boards L and M using glue and 1½" screws. Drive the screws from the inside to secure the boards.

You can easily cut the 45° angles on your table saw by making a cutting sled. It's simply a piece of ½" plywood with a ¾" wood cleat running in the miter gauge tracks. The sled fence is set to 45° and secured in place.

10 Follow the Materials List and prepare the two stiles R, and two rails S for the upper face frame, which is assembled using the same techniques as the lower frame. Notice that the rails are 1½" high for this frame assembly. Attach the face frame to the upper carcass using biscuits and glue.

9 Cut the upper backs N and P, and the two sides Q. Follow the same procedures when building the upper carcass that were used for the lower case. Use glue and biscuits, dowels or screws when assembling the carcass, making sure the joints are at 90° to each other.

12 Sand the middle board, then round over the upper and lower edges of the hardwood face. Use a ⅜"-radius roundover bit in your router.

11 Trace the middle fixed shelf pattern on a piece of ¾"-thick veneer plywood using the template. This shelf T is cut ⅜" inside the trace lines on the side and front edges, U and V. The back edges are cut on the template lines. Use biscuits to attach a hardwood edge that's 1¼" wide to the sides and front edges. Join the corners with 22.5° angles and clamp until the adhesive is set.

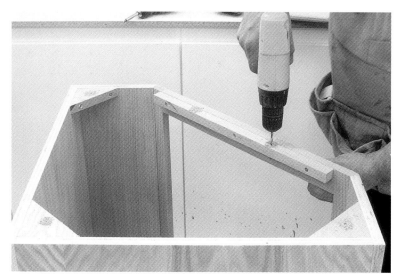

13 Attach the wood cleat W to the back face of the lower face frame top rail. Secure it flush with the rail's top edge. Use glue and 1¼" screws to secure the cleat. Drill through pilot holes in the cleat and three corner blocks for screws to attach the upper section.

14 Secure the middle fixed shelf T to the bottom of the upper section using glue and 2" screws. Align this board with its two back edges flush with the back faces of the upper section back boards.

15 Use the template to trace another pattern on a ¾"-thick veneer plywood panel. This will be the top board X for the upper carcass. The board is cut following the template trace lines. Attach it to the cabinet with all edges flush to the outside faces of the upper carcass. Use glue and 2" screws.

16 Attach the upper cabinet section to the lower cabinet. Use glue and 1¼"-long screws through the cleat W and corner blocks D to secure the sections. Attach the upper and lower carcass making sure their backs are aligned.

17 | The top moulding Y and Z has been designed to match existing furniture. However, any style of moulding can be used. I have attached a ¾"-square cleat to the back side of a ¾"-thick by 3"-high hardwood board with rounded edges. Screws have been used in pilot holes to secure the moulding on the cabinet.

18 | Cut a shelf hole jig 36" long for the upper section, and 30" long for the lower section. Drill a row of pilot holes in the jig spaced 2" apart. Drill through the center of a wood dowel and leave it on the drill bit to act as a stop to limit the holes' depth. Drill holes in the back and side panels for the shelf pins you plan to use. I used $5/16$"-diameter solid brass pins.

Making the Cabinet Doors

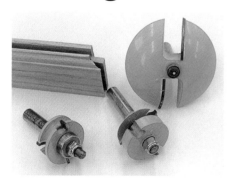

To make cope-and-stick doors for this cabinet you will need a rail-and-stile cutter set for your router, as well as a panel-raising bit if you decide to make a solid raised panel for the lower door. A rail-and-stile width of 2¼" is common and can be used for all rail-and-stile cutter sets. However, the rail length depends on the profile or depth of cut for your set. Don't use my rail length dimensions until you verify the size needed for your cutters to produce a 19"-wide door. Building these doors requires extra attention to detail because of the inset style. The front faces of the doors are flush with the front face of the face frame. To achieve the ¹⁄₁₆" gap around the perimeter of the doors the process demands accurately cut square doors, so take your time and double-check each step.

19 | The upper door will be a cope-and-stick frame with a glass center panel. The lower door will have a solid raised panel. Calculate your rail and stile sizes for your bit set and build the doors to the exact inside opening dimension of the upper and lower face frame. The doors will be trimmed afterwards for the ¹⁄₁₆" gap. First, cut all the edge profiles on the stiles and rails, DD, EE, FF and GG, for both doors.

20 | Cut the rail ends with the cope bit. Always test cut a piece of scrap before making the final cut with these bit sets.

21 | My bit set does not cut the bottom edge of the stiles and rails to accept a glass panel and rubber gasket. If your bit set is like mine and you want to use the rubber gasket method, cut ¼" off the back section of each stile and rail. The rails can be cut through, but the stile cuts must be stopped 2" short of the end.

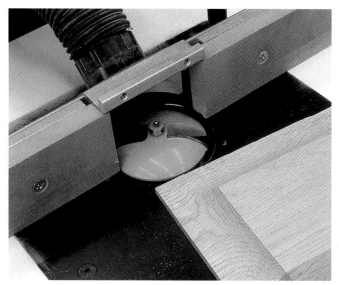

22 | The lower door can be fitted with a ¼"-thick plywood veneer panel or a solid raised panel. I used a raising bit to cut my center panel from a glued-up block of boards that were ¾" thick. My stiles and rails are ¾" thick so the panel will sit "proud" of the frame surface. If I wanted a center panel flush with the frame I would cut a ⅝"-thick panel. Either option is acceptable and depends on the look you prefer.

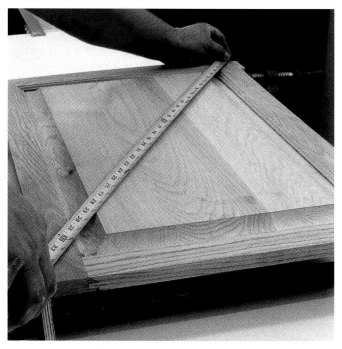

23 | Assemble both upper and lower doors. Do not glue the lower door's panel in place, as it must be free to move with changes in humidity. Glue is used on the stile-and-rail joints only. Check the diagonal corners of the doors after securing with clamps to ensure the door is square. If the distances are equal, the door is square. Correct any errors by lightly tapping on the longer diagonal until both are equal.

24 I have used a rubber gasket designed specifically for securing glass panels in cope-and-stick doors. However, there are many ways to install the glass, including clips and silicone adhesive.

25 There are also dozens of hinge options for the doors. Your choice depends on the style of cabinet, other furnishings in the room and personal taste. I used a traditional hinge that doesn't require a mortise because it folds into itself. It is also $\frac{1}{16}$" thick, which is the spacing I require around my inset door. There should be a $\frac{1}{16}$" gap around the perimeter of each door. Trial fit the doors and plane or sand them to achieve the perfect fit.

26 Select your handles, latch and lamp assembly. I used a plain knob to match the hinge finish, and a small magnetic catch. The lamp is a quartz halogen fixture with a built-in switch.

construction NOTES

Complete the cabinet by sanding all the surfaces and applying a finish. My cabinet has a custom stain and three coats of polyurethane. For increased protection and a smooth finish, I applied a coat of hard clear paste wax with #0000 steel wool.

As I previously mentioned, this corner cabinet is trimmed in a contemporary style. But you can change the cabinet style to traditional, classic or any other by simply installing a different top and base moulding. The basic case construction is the same no matter which style you choose.

This cabinet size suits my requirements. The dimensions in the Materials List are only a guide. Alter the height, back board width or opening to suit your needs.

The design calls for $\frac{3}{4}$"-thick plywood veneer for the case construction. It's an expensive sheet material, but one that's strong and well worth using for this project. The use of this material eliminates the need for added structural support frames, so in this case it is cost effective.

You might consider another design change. The upper section side boards may be replaced with a wooden frame to support a glass panel. It's dramatically different and increases the view inside the upper display area. If you have a collection that requires maximum exposure, glass side panels might be the solution.

wine display and storage cabinet

Home wine making has recently become a very popular hobby. I visited one of the wine supply stores in my village and was surprised to see the number of wine batches waiting to be bottled. I also learned that the storage and display of these finished wines is always a problem. Most batches of wine fill from 20 to 30 bottles, and unless you have a wine cellar you have to consider where those bottles will be stored.

THIS PROJECT HIGHLIGHTS a number of woodworking techniques. The sides are prepared by cutting rabbets and dadoes, biscuit joinery is used to attach the face frame and I have also detailed cutting chamfers on the table saw.

This project has two doors and a drawer face that are made using the table saw. You don't need a fancy router table or expensive bit set to make these popular and solid raised-panel doors. All you need is a decent table saw and a little patience.

The sides are ¾" veneer plywood and the back board is ½" veneer particleboard. The face

frame and bottle racks are made with solid wood, creating a beautiful end result. This cabinet will be a welcomed addition to any home. I suspect you'll make more than one when your wine-making friends see the finished project.

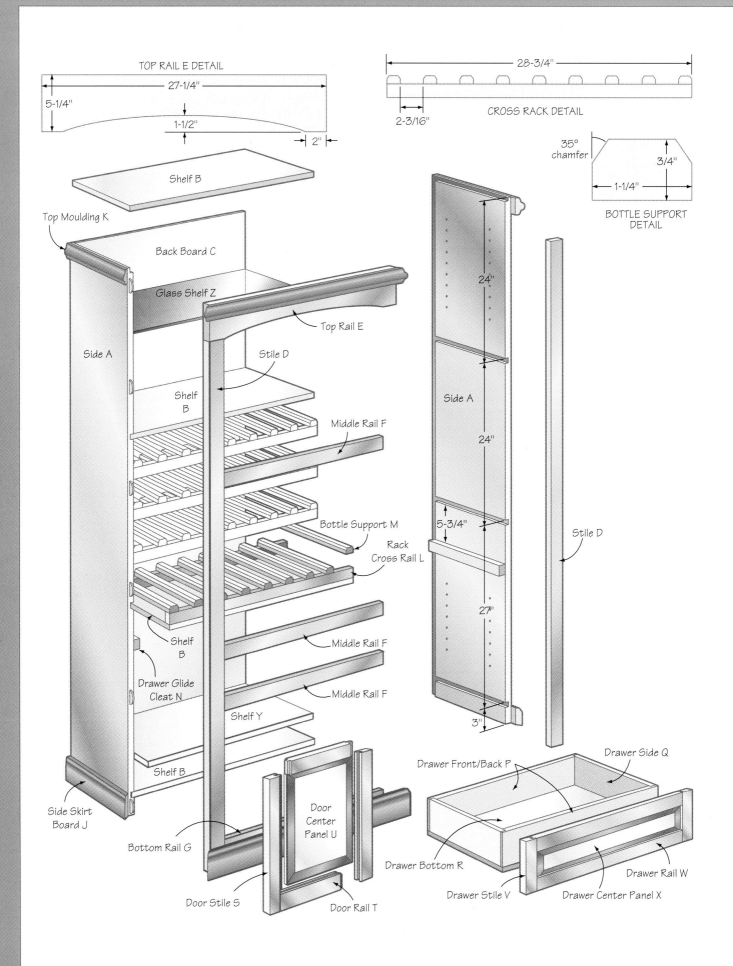

TOP RAIL E DETAIL

27-1/4"

5-1/4"

1-1/2"

2"

28-3/4"

CROSS RACK DETAIL

2-3/16"

35° chamfer

3/4"

1-1/4"

BOTTLE SUPPORT DETAIL

Shelf B

Top Moulding K

Back Board C

Glass Shelf Z

Top Rail E

Side A

Stile D

Shelf B

Middle Rail F

24"

Side A

24"

Bottle Support M

Rack Cross Rail L

5-3/4"

Shelf B

Stile D

Drawer Glide Cleat N

Middle Rail F

27"

Middle Rail F

Shelf Y

3"

Shelf B

Side Skirt Board J

Bottom Rail G

Door Center Panel U

Door Stile S

Door Rail T

Drawer Front/Back P

Drawer Side Q

Drawer Bottom R

Drawer Stile V

Drawer Rail W

Drawer Center Panel X

materials list | **inches**

REFERENCE	QUANTITY	PART	STOCK	THICKNESS	WIDTH	LENGTH	COMMENTS
A	2	sides	oak pw*	3/4	14	78	
B	4	fixed shelves	oak pw	3/4	13 1/2	29 1/2	
C	1	back board	vp**	1/2	29 1/2	75 3/4	
D	2	stiles	oak	3/4	1 1/2	78	
E	1	top rail	oak	3/4	5 1/4	27 1/4	
F	3	middle rails	oak	3/4	1 1/2	27 1/4	
G	1	bottom rail	oak	3/4	3	27 1/4	
H	1	front skirt board	oak	3/4	3	31 3/4	A
J	2	side skirt boards	oak	3/4	3	15 1/2	B
K	1	top moulding	oak			96	
L	8	rack cross rails	oak	3/4	1 1/4	28 3/4	
M	36	bottle supports	oak	3/4	1 1/4	13 1/2	C
N	2	drawer glide cleats	oak	3/4	1 1/2	13 1/2	
P	2	drawer fronts & backs	bp***	1/2	3 1/2	26 1/4	
Q	2	drawer sides	bp	1/2	3 1/2	11 1/2	
R	1	drawer bottom	bp	1/2	12	26 1/4	

Doors

S	4	stiles	oak	3/4	2 1/4	20 1/4	
T	4	rails	oak	3/4	2 1/4	10 5/8	
U	2	center panels	oak	3/4	10 3/8	16 3/8	D

Drawer Face

V	2	stiles	oak	3/4	2 1/4	6	
W	2	rails	oak	3/4	1 1/2	10 5/8	
X	1	center panel	oak	3/4	3 5/8	24 1/2	D
Y	1	lower section shelf	oak pw	3/4	13 3/8	28 1/2	
Z	1	upper section shelf	glass	1/4	13 3/8	28 1/2	E

  *plywood
 **veneered particleboard
***birch plywood

A: angle cut on both ends
B: angle cut on one end
C: chamfered on top edges
D: raised panel
E: tempered with polished edges

materials list | **millimeters**

REFERENCE	QUANTITY	PART	STOCK	THICKNESS	WIDTH	LENGTH	COMMENTS
A	2	sides	oak pw*	19	356	1981	
B	4	fixed shelves	oak pw	19	343	750	
C	1	back board	vp**	13	750	1924	
D	2	stiles	oak	19	38	1981	
E	1	top rail	oak	19	133	692	
F	3	middle rails	oak	19	38	692	
G	1	bottom rail	oak	19	76	692	
H	1	front skirt board	oak	19	76	806	A
J	2	side skirt boards	oak	19	76	394	B
K	1	top moulding	oak			2438	
L	8	rack cross rails	oak	19	32	730	
M	36	bottle supports	oak	19	32	343	C
N	2	drawer glide cleats	oak	19	32	343	
P	2	drawer fronts & backs	bp***	13	89	666	
Q	2	drawer sides	bp	13	89	292	
R	1	drawer bottom	bp	13	305	666	

Doors

S	4	stiles	oak	19	57	514	
T	4	rails	oak	19	57	270	
U	2	center panels	oak	19	264	416	D

Drawer Face

V	2	stiles	oak	19	57	152	
W	2	rails	oak	19	38	270	
X	1	center panel	oak	19	92	623	D
Y	1	lower section shelf	oak pw	19	340	724	
Z	1	upper section shelf	glass	6	340	724	E

  *plywood
 **veneered particleboard
***birch plywood

A: angle cut on both ends
B: angle cut on one end
C: chamfered on top edges
D: raised panel
E: tempered with polished edges

Building the Wine Cabinet

1 Cut the two side panels A as detailed in the Materials List. Prepare the sides for assembly by routering the dadoes and rabbets, as shown. All the cuts are ³⁄₈" deep. The horizontal dadoes and rabbets are ¾" wide and the back rabbets are ½" wide to accept the back board. Use a ¾" router bit and straight-edged guide to make the cuts.

2 Cut the four fixed shelves B. Spread glue in the horizontal dadoes and rabbets on both side panels. Install the shelves and clamp the cabinet sides, making sure the assembly is square. Leave the cabinet clamped until the adhesive sets.

3 The back board C is a ½"-thick piece of veneer particleboard. Cut it to the size listed, noting that it isn't as long as the cabinet sides. The back board is installed in the rabbets and aligned flush with the top edge of the side boards. Use glue in the rabbets and finishing or brad nails to secure this panel. If the back board is accurately cut, the case will be square.

4 Attach one stile D using glue and No. 20 biscuits or dowels. If you don't have either joinery system, you can face nail the stile in place. The outside edge of the stile is flush with the outside face of the side board. Clamp the stile in place while the adhesive sets. Align the opposite stile but don't glue it at this time. It can be temporarily held with clamps.

tip

If possible, clamp both sides of a cabinet together when cutting dadoes and rabbets. Cutting both sides at the same time, along a straight-edged guide, ensures perfect mirror image sides.

5 The top rail E has a decorative arc and is formed using a 5¼"-wide board. Mark points that are 2" in from each end of the board, and make a center mark that's 1½" above the bottom edge. The arc can be drawn by bending a thin strip of wood around finishing nails driven into the waste area of the arc. Cut the arc using a band saw or jigsaw. This rail design adds visual interest to the cabinet and is high enough to hide a lamp fixture. Attach this rail with biscuits or dowels and dry fit it in place.

6 Cut and dry fit the remaining rails F and G using biscuits or dowels. Note that all rails are installed with their top edges flush with the top face of the shelf they cover. The drawer rail is attached leaving a 5" space for the drawer box. This rail doesn't cover a shelf and must be installed with dowels or pocket-hole screws and glue. Dry fit all the rails and remaining stile. When the fit is correct, apply glue and clamp securely. Refer to the illustration for correct positioning of all face frame parts.

7 Sand the face frame smooth and check all of the joints. Use a ⅜" roundover bit in a router to ease the inside perimeter of the two upper sections. Don't round over the outside edges of the cabinet at this time.

tip

It's difficult to clamp the rails to the shelf edge on a case with a back board installed. You can buy specialized clamps or create your own inexpensive clamping tool using wedged cedar shims. Install a pipe clamp across the cabinet, directly over the rail to be clamped. The pipe should be ⅛" above the rail surface. Drive cedar shims between the pipe and rail face until the joint is tight. Leave the shims in place until the glue sets. Refer to the image in step 6.

8 Cut and install a base skirt on the front and both sides. The three boards H and J are joined at the corners with 45° miters. Use glue and 1¼"-long screws from the inside of the cabinet to secure the boards. The 3"-high skirt boards are attached 1" below the top edge of the bottom rail. The top edge of these boards can be decorated with a cove, roundover, or Roman ogee cut. Any design is suitable, it's a matter of personal taste and depends a great deal on the furniture in the room where this cabinet will be placed. These skirt boards were cut with a cove bit.

9 The top moulding K is another design choice. I'm using a commercial profile that's available at most lumberyards. One 8' length of moulding will be enough to trim the top.

tip

You can choose from hundreds of moulding options for your cabinet top. The look can be dramatically altered with a simple change of moulding, so try a number of styles until you find one that suits your taste. Here is a classic traditional style with a head cap that's been rounded over and a 3" crown moulding. The crown is a stock lumberyard moulding.

10 Once the base skirt and top moulding are installed the outside edges of the stiles can be rounded over. Use a ⅜" roundover bit in a router. The router plate will be stopped by both the base and top trim, which will define the cut distance.

Building the Wine Rack

11 Cut the cross rails L as well as the 36 bottle supports M. These supports are cut with a chamfer on two edges using a table saw. Set the fence 1" away from the blade at 35°.

12 Assemble the racks using glue and brad nails. If you use standard finishing nails drill a pilot hole to avoid splitting the supports. A $2^3/16$"-wide spacer will help align the supports. Check each rack assembly with a square before the glue sets and adjust if necessary. Fill the nail holes and finish sand each rack before installing into the cabinet.

14 Drill adjustable shelf pin holes in the top and bottom sections. Select the shelf pins before drilling to determine the correct diameter for the hole. Make a jig to drill the holes. A length of dowel rod on the bit can be used as a stop to limit hole depth.

13 Install the wine racks in the cabinet, beginning with the bottom assembly. Use 1" screws through the back board into the rear cross rails. The front cross rails are attached to the face frame stiles with $1^1/4$"-long screws. Use two $4^1/4$"-high spacers to hold the racks at the correct height during the installation. The distance from the bottom of one cross rail to the bottom of the cross rail directly above should be $5^1/2$". All of the racks should be loosely installed inside the cabinet before securing them, otherwise you won't be able to get the last rack in the cabinet.

tip

Driving screws through a back board into an assembly is tricky. It's easy to miss your mark without a great deal of measuring. Fortunately there is a simpler method. First, set the rack in place and lightly mark its position against the back board with a pencil. Remove the rack and drill pilot holes from the front through the back. When the rack is put back in place you'll have perfectly aligned guide holes on the blind side for the screws.

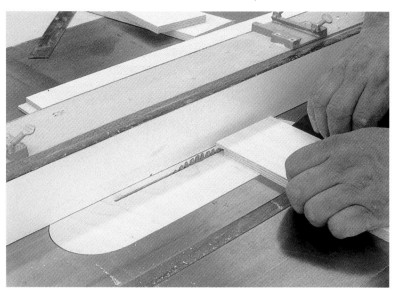

15 Cut and install the two drawer cleats N. They are attached with glue and 1¼"-long screws. The cleats are aligned with the top edge of the bottom drawer rail.

16 The drawer box is 1" less in height and width. This rule can be used for most of the drawer glides that are available today. All of the five drawer boards, P, Q and R, are ½"-thick Baltic birch. The layers are void-free making this material a popular choice when building drawer boxes. The front and back boards require ¼"-deep by ½"-wide rabbets on each end. These cuts are quickly made using a table saw.

17 Assemble the drawer box using glue and brad nails. The sides Q fit into the front and back board rabbets.

18 Install the drawer box on 12"-long full-extension side-mounted drawer glides. My glides are manufactured by Accuride, but a number of other manufacturers sell this hardware.

Building Raised-Panel Doors and Drawers

19 The raised-panel doors, S, T and U, and drawer face, V, W and X, will be made using the table saw. First calculate the door size. When using hidden European-style hinges, add 1" to the door opening width and divide by two for two doors. If you're making a cabinet with one door, the interior width plus 1" is the final door size. The opening width, from inside stile edge to inside stile edge, is 7¼". I need two doors so my door width will be 14⅛" (27¼" plus 1" divided by two). Remember to use the smallest interior dimension. In this case the stile-to-stile width is less than the side-to-side width, so we will use the smaller, stile-to-stile, dimension. The door height can be any dimension as long as it overlaps the upper and lower rail by at least ¼". The drawer face is normally 1" higher and wider than the opening, so it's 6"-high by 28¼"-wide. Cut all the stiles and rails for the doors and drawer face. Each one requires a ¼"-wide by ½"-deep groove on one edge. Use the table saw to complete this step.

20 All the rails require a ¼"-thick by ½"-long tenon centered on both ends. Use the miter gauge on your table saw to cut these tenons.

21 Glue up enough ¾"-thick boards to make two doors and one drawer center panel, X. Clamp a straight-edged hardwood board across the table saw blade. Use the miter slide to align the board 90° across the center of the saw blade when it's fully lowered. Raise the blade ¹⁄₃₂" and run all four sides of each panel over the blade slowly. Repeat this step until the panel fits snugly, but is not binding, in the stile and rail grooves. Take it slowly and be careful because the blade is exposed.

Raising narrow panels is difficult because they tend to rock as the cuts get deeper. To stop this rocking and get clean, uniform cuts, screw guide boards on the panel that can be slid along the saw's guide board.

22 Assemble the two doors and drawer face using glue on the tenons only. Do not glue the center panels, so they can float during expansion and contraction of the wood. Clamp the three assemblies as the floating panels sometimes rattle. To prevent this I use small pieces of door weather stripping, a common soft foam strip that's available in hardware stores. Put a couple of strips in each groove before inserting the panels. Once the adhesive has set, sand the assemblies and round over the front face edges with a $\frac{3}{8}$" roundover router bit.

23 Drill two 35mm-diameter holes in each door, $\frac{1}{8}$" from the edge. I normally space my hinge holes 4" from the top and bottom. The doors will be mounted with hidden hinges, but we can't use the standard cabinet side mounting plate. The stiles are further into the interior cabinet space than the sides, so a face frame mounting plate has been used. I mount doors with the mounting plate attached, holding them in their open position, with a $\frac{1}{8}$"-thick spacer between the stile face and door. However, face frame mounting plates have two "nibs" that make them self-aligning. The face frame mounting plate is the lower piece of hardware in the illustration.

24 Attach the drawer front using two 1¼"-long screws from the inside. The simplest way to align the drawer face on the box is to select the handle you will be using and drill holes in the drawer face only. Hold the face in place and drive screws through the handle holes to temporarily secure the drawer face. Open the drawer and attach the face permanently using screws from inside the drawer box. Finally, remove the screws in the handle holes and drill through the drawer box. Install the handles after a finish has been applied.

25 Cut the lower plywood veneer shelf Y and apply iron-on wood tape to the outside edge. Order a tempered glass shelf Z with polished edges and prepare to apply a finish to your cabinet.

construction NOTES

I completed the sanding on my cabinet and applied three coats of oil-based polyurethane.

Then I installed a fluorescent fixture with a built-in switch. There are many styles of cabinet fixtures available in different price ranges; select one that suits your taste and budget.

I've used oak because it's reasonably priced and common to my area. However, any wood species can be used. I like the ¾" plywood veneer sheets, but they can be expensive. Using ¹¹⁄₁₆"- or ¾"-thick particleboard veneer is perfectly acceptable if you want to lower the construction cost a little.

As previously mentioned, the cabinet style can be changed from contemporary to traditional with top and base moulding designs. The cabinet width, height and depth are dimensions I chose; they may not be suitable for your needs so change them as desired.

The cabinet construction style of this project is simple and flexible. It is a common building method and can be easily changed. I have an upper section with glass shelves, a middle section with wine racks, a drawer and lower door section. It can be built with display shelves in place of the racks, doors in the center section, a drop-leaf front for a bar and full glass shelving. The design possibilities are endless.

entertainment and display cabinet

THIS CABINET IS LESS THAN 4' high, so the top can be used to display photographs. There are even three drawers in the base for videotapes, compact discs or audiotape storage.

The cabinet was constructed using ¾"-thick maple veneer particleboard and solid maple hardwood. The stain is a custom color to match existing furniture.

Maple is a dense hardwood, so it's not surprising that this cabinet is very heavy. Nevertheless, special attention was paid to reinforcing the middle shelf because of its span and the load that a large television would place on that board. The television section of the cabinet is able to accommodate a 27" unit. However, I suggest you measure your TV before cutting any material to be sure of your requirements.

This entertainment and display cabinet can be used to show off many different types of collectibles. The adjustable shelves are adaptable, and since the cabinet must be deep for the television there's a large top to display your family photos.

Blanche Gale of Ottawa, Ontario, owns the lovely and interesting collection of family treasures displayed at the right.

There isn't always enough space in a room for both a dedicated display cabinet and an entertainment unit. This project combines these two popular cabinets into one, providing space for a television as well as ample shelving for your treasured collectibles.

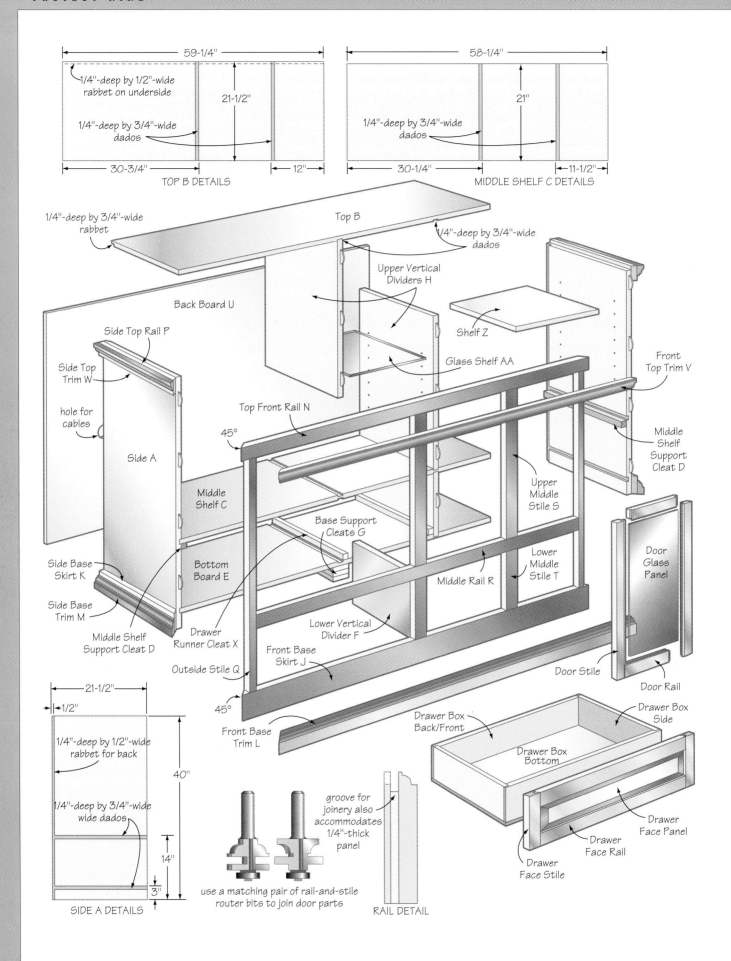

TOP B DETAILS

59-1/4"

1/4"-deep by 1/2"-wide rabbet on underside

1/4"-deep by 3/4"-wide dados

21-1/2"

30-3/4"

12"

MIDDLE SHELF C DETAILS

58-1/4"

1/4"-deep by 3/4"-wide dados

21"

30-1/4"

11-1/2"

1/4"-deep by 3/4"-wide rabbet

Top B

1/4"-deep by 3/4"-wide dados

Back Board U

Upper Vertical Dividers H

Shelf Z

Side Top Rail P

Side Top Trim W

Glass Shelf AA

Front Top Trim V

hole for cables

Top Front Rail N

45°

Middle Shelf Support Cleat D

Side A

Upper Middle Stile S

Middle Shelf C

Base Support Cleats G

Lower Middle Stile T

Side Base Skirt K

Bottom Board E

Middle Rail R

Door Glass Panel

Side Base Trim M

Middle Shelf Support Cleat D

Drawer Runner Cleat X

Lower Vertical Divider F

Outside Stile Q

Front Base Skirt J

Door Stile

Door Rail

45°

Front Base Trim L

Drawer Box Back/Front

Drawer Box Side

Drawer Box Bottom

Drawer Face Panel

Drawer Face Rail

Drawer Face Stile

SIDE A DETAILS

21-1/2"

1/2"

1/4"-deep by 1/2"-wide rabbet for back

1/4"-deep by 3/4"-wide wide dados

40"

14"

3"

use a matching pair of rail-and-stile router bits to join door parts

groove for joinery also accommodates 1/4"-thick panel

RAIL DETAIL

materials list | inches

REFERENCE	QUANTITY	PART	STOCK	THICKNESS	WIDTH	LENGTH	COMMENTS
A	2	sides	oak	$3/4$	$21^{1}/_2$	40	
B	1	top	oak	$3/4$	$21^{1}/_2$	$59^{1}/_4$	
C	1	middle shelf	oak	$3/4$	21	$58^{1}/_4$	
D	2	middle shelf support cleats	oak	$3/4$	1	21	
E	1	bottom board	oak	$3/4$	21	$58^{1}/_4$	
F	2	lower vertical dividers	oak	$3/4$	$10^{1}/_4$	21	
G	3	base support cleats	oak	$3/4$	3	21	
H	2	upper vertical dividers	oak	$3/4$	$26^{1}/_2$	21	
J	1	front base skirt	oak	$3/4$	3	$60^{3}/_4$	A
K	2	side base skirts	oak	$3/4$	3	$22^{1}/_4$	B
L	1	front base trim	oak	$3/4$	$1^{1}/_2$	$62^{1}/_2$	A
M	2	side base trim	oak	$3/4$	$1^{1}/_2$	23	B
N	1	top front rail	oak	$3/4$	2	$60^{3}/_4$	A
P	2	side top rails	oak	$3/4$	2	$22^{1}/_4$	B
Q	2	outside stiles	oak	$3/4$	$3/4$	$35^{3}/_4$	
R	1	middle rail	oak	$3/4$	$1^{1}/_2$	$57^{3}/_4$	
S	2	upper middle stiles	oak	$3/4$	$1^{1}/_2$	$24^{3}/_4$	
T	2	lower middle stiles	oak	$3/4$	$1^{1}/_2$	$9^{1}/_2$	
U	1	back board	oak	$1/2$	38	$58^{1}/_4$	
V	1	front top trim	oak	$3/4$	$1^{1}/_4$	$62^{1}/_4$	A
W	2	side top trim	oak	$3/4$	$1^{1}/_4$	23	B
X	2	drawer runner cleats	oak	$3/4$	$1^{1}/_2$	18	
Y	1	television section shelf	oak	$3/4$	$20^{3}/_4$	$29^{1}/_8$	
Z	2	right-hand upper section shelf	oak	$3/4$	$10^{3}/_8$	$20^{3}/_4$	
AA	2	center section shelves	glass	$1/4$	$16^{3}/_8$	$20^{3}/_4$	

Drawer Boxes

The drawer boxes are $8^{1}/_2$"-high by 18"-deep. The three finished widths are $9^{1}/_2$" wide, 14" wide, and $28^{1}/_4$" wide.

BB	6	sides	Baltic bp*	$1/2$	8	18	
CC	2	backs/fronts	Baltic bp	$1/2$	8	9	
DD	1	bottom	Baltic bp	$1/2$	$9^{1}/_2$	18	
EE	2	backs/fronts	Baltic bp	$1/2$	8	$13^{1}/_2$	
FF	1	bottom	Baltic bp	$1/2$	14	18	
GG	2	backs/fronts	Baltic bp	$1/2$	8	$27^{3}/_4$	
HH	1	bottom	Baltic bp	$1/2$	$28^{1}/_4$	18	

Drawer Faces

JJ	1	right drawer face	oak	$3/4$	$10^{1}/_2$	$11^{1}/_2$	
KK	1	center drawer face	oak	$3/4$	$10^{1}/_2$	16	
LL	1	left drawer face	oak	$3/4$	$10^{1}/_2$	$30^{1}/_4$	

Glass Door Frame

MM	1		oak	$3/4$	16	26	
NN	1		glass	$1/4$	to fit		

*Baltic birch plywood

A: angled at 45° on both ends

B: angled at 45° on the front end

materials list | millimeters

REFERENCE	QUANTITY	PART	STOCK	THICKNESS	WIDTH	LENGTH	COMMENTS
A	2	sides	oak	19	546	1016	
B	1	top	oak	19	546	1505	
C	1	middle shelf	oak	19	533	1479	
D	3	middle shelf support cleats	oak	19	25	533	
E	1	bottom board	oak	19	533	1479	
F	2	lower vertical dividers	oak	19	260	533	
G	3	base support cleats	oak	19	76	533	
H	2	upper vertical dividers	oak	19	673	533	
J	1	front base skirt	oak	19	76	1543	A
K	2	side base skirts	oak	19	76	565	B
L	1	front base trim	oak	19	38	1588	A
M	2	side base trim	oak	19	38	584	B
N	1	top front rail	oak	19	51	1543	A
P	2	side top rails	oak	19	51	565	B
Q	2	outside stiles	oak	19	19	908	
R	1	middle rail	oak	19	38	1467	
S	2	upper middle stiles	oak	19	38	629	
T	2	lower middle stiles	oak	19	38	242	
U	1	back board	oak	13	965	1479	
V	1	front top trim	oak	19	32	1581	A
W	2	side top trim	oak	19	32	584	B
X	2	drawer runner cleats	oak	19	38	457	
Y	1	television section shelf	oak	19	521	740	
Z	2	right-hand upper section shelf	oak	19	264	527	
AA	2	center section shelves	glass	6	416	527	

Drawer Boxes

The drawer boxes are 216mm-high by 457mm-deep. The three finished widths are 242mm, 356mm and 717mm wide.

BB	6	sides	Baltic bp*	13	203	457	
CC	2	backs/fronts	Baltic bp	13	203	229	
DD	1	bottom	Baltic bp	13	242	457	
EE	2	backs/fronts	Baltic bp	13	203	343	
FF	1	bottom	Baltic bp	13	356	457	
GG	2	backs/fronts	Baltic bp	13	203	705	
HH	1	bottom	Baltic bp	13	717	457	

Drawer Faces

JJ	1	right drawer face	oak	19	267	292	
KK	1	center drawer face	oak	19	267	406	
LL	1	left drawer face	oak	19	267	768	

Glass Door Frame

MM	1		oak	19	406	660	
NN	1		glass	6	to fit		

*Baltic birch plywood

A: angled at 45° on both ends

B: angled at 45° on the front end

Building the Entertainment and Display Cabinet

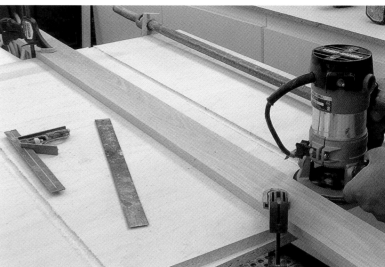

1 Prepare the two sides A by cutting to size and routering two ¾"-wide by ¼"-deep dadoes. These sides also require a ½"-wide by ¼"-inch deep rabbet on the back inside face. Use a ¾" straight router bit in a handheld router to form the cuts. Clamp the two sides together when routering mirror image panels to ensure perfect alignment of the cuts.

2 Cut the top B and middle shelf C to size, as detailed in the Materials List. Form the ¾"-wide by ¼"-deep dadoes in each panel, making sure they are oriented properly. Note that the dado positions on both boards are different with respect to the end dimension. They can be clamped together when cutting the dadoes if the top is positioned ½" beyond both ends of the middle shelf. The depth of top A is greater because it's flush with the back edge of the side panel. The middle shelf is narrower so the back board butts tightly to the back edge. Cut a ½"-wide by ¼"-deep rabbet on the rear underside face of the top board to accept the back board.

3 The cabinet requires two support cleats D to strengthen the middle shelf, as it will support a lot of weight. Cut the cleats to size and drill through holes in them so the screws will turn freely, drawing the cleats tight. These 1"-wide cleats will be secured with glue and screws, and are aligned with the bottom edge of the middle dado on each side board. They will be hidden by the face frame and should be mounted flush with the front edge of the side panel. The ½" space at the back end will allow installation of the back panel. Install one cleat per side panel at this time.

4 Attach the middle shelf C to the side panels in the dadoes. Secure with glue and screws through the support cleats. The middle shelf should be aligned flush with the front edge of each side panel.

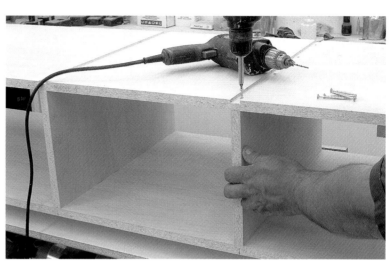

5 The bottom board E is installed in the lower dadoes of each side panel. Use glue and screws through the outside face of the side boards. The base skirt will hide these screw heads.

6 Cut and install the two lower dividers F. Use glue and 2"-long screws in piloted holes. The dividers are aligned with the dadoes on the middle shelf. Align them vertically and install screws through the dadoes on the top side of the middle shelf, and through the bottom board in the divider edges.

8 Attach the cabinet top to the side panels. Use biscuits, or dowels and glue, then clamp in place. The ends of this top board are flush with the outside faces of the side boards.

7 The bottom board needs a center base support G to help support the load of a television. The support is 2¼" thick. Three pieces of 3"-wide shop scraps that are ¾" thick can be used. I've made my support with three lengths of particleboard cutoffs. This support will not be seen, so just about any ¾" material can be used. Center this support under the lower middle divider. Use glue and screws to install the support cleat.

9 Attach a middle shelf support cleat D on the center lower divider panel. The cleat will strengthen the middle shelf to help support the television load. Use glue and screws to secure the cleat.

10 The two upper vertical dividers H can now be installed. Set the panels in the dadoes on both the top and middle shelves after applying glue to the joints. Clamp the dividers in place with their front edges flush to the front edges of the top and middle boards.

11 Use a piece of plywood or particleboard that's 21"-wide by 26"-high to make a drill jig. Drill two rows of holes that are the same diameter as the adjustable shelf pins you plan to use. I used $^5/_{16}$"-diameter pins and spaced the holes $1^1/_4$" apart. Clamp the jig to the vertical panels that require holes, and use a drill bit with a wooden dowel stop to limit the hole depth. You may want to stagger the columns of holes in the center section to avoid aligning with holes in the right and left sections if you are drilling deeper than $^1/_4$".

12 Normally, a back board would be installed at this point. However I want to use biscuits to secure the face frame members, and clamping through the carcass is the best way to proceed. First, prepare the three base skirt boards J and K. These 3"-high boards are mitered at the corners to wrap around the carcass. Verify the dimensions on your unit before cutting the miters. The skirt boards don't have a decorative profile because the bottom drawer faces are overlaid. Attach the boards with glue and biscuits, then clamp securely making sure the top edge is flush with the upper face of the bottom board. If you don't have a biscuit joiner, use cleats or brackets with glue on the back face, and clamp until the glue cures.

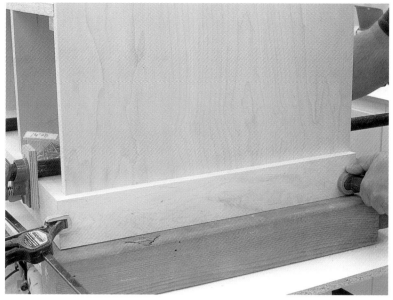

13 The two side base skirt boards K are attached with glue and screws through the rear face of the side panels.

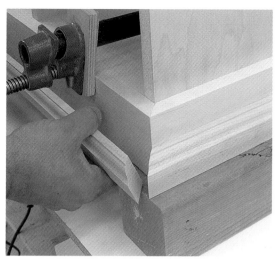

14 A decorative base shoe L and M is used around the perimeter of the base skirt. Use any trim style that's suitable, but limit the height to 1½". Secure the trim with glue and screws through the rear face of the base skirt. I used a Roman ogee bit in a table-mounted router to create my trim.

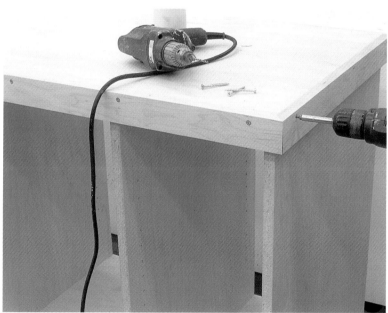

15 The top edge of the carcass is wrapped with a 2"-high solid wood band. The front and both sides are covered. The wood can be attached with glue and screws through the face as the screw heads will be covered with the same style of trim that was used for the base shoe. Miter the corners at 45° and use a pilot hole before installing the 2" screws.

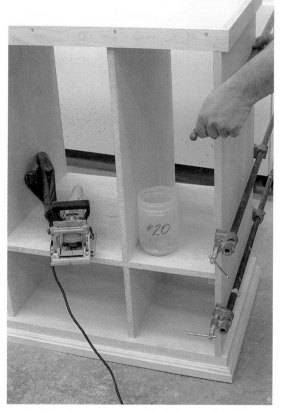

16 The stiles and middle rail will be installed before the top trim. It's important to follow these steps because some of the openings will be rounded over, and the trim will limit the router travel. Cut the two outside stiles Q and attach them with glue and biscuits or finishing nails.

17 Cut and attach the middle rail R with glue and #20 biscuits. The top edge of this rail is aligned flush with the top surface of the middle shelf. If you don't have a biscuit joiner secure the frame members with glue and finishing nails.

18 Install the last four stiles S and T. These stiles are 1½" wide and installed so they extend ¾" into the center section. The upper, center section door is installed with hidden hinges and face frame mounting plates on the stiles. The hinges leave a reveal of approximately ¾" on each side of the glass panel door, balancing the look of the outside stiles.

19 The back board U can be installed at this point, as all the through clamping is done. The ½"-thick veneer particleboard back is installed in the side and top panel rabbets and secured with glue and finishing nails.

20 Now is the perfect time to finish sand the face frame. Use a ⅜" roundover router bit to ease the inside edges of the face frame on the two outside upper sections. The middle upper, as well as the three lower sections, will be covered.

21 The upper trim V and W is the same pattern as the base shoe trim, but the height is reduced to 1¼". Attach the trim with glue and biscuits, or face nail flush with the top edge banding. Miter the corners at 45° on both corners.

22 Sand the top smooth, being careful not to penetrate the veneer layer. Use a ⅜" roundover bit to ease the top edge of the trim.

Building the Doors and Drawer Faces

24 The cabinet runners of the bottom-mounted drawer glides must be installed flush with the inside edges of the stiles to operate correctly. The lower middle section requires two ¾"-thick cleats that are 1½" high to position and support the glides. Attach the cleats X with glue and 1¼" screws.

23 The drawers are constructed with ½"-thick Baltic birch cabinet grade plywood. The drawer box size is 1" less than the opening height and width when using bottom-mounted drawer glides. Cut the drawer parts as detailed in the Materials List. Each side panel requires a ¼"-deep by ½"-wide rabbet on the inside face of both ends. The front and back boards will be attached in these rabbets with glue and finishing nails. All drawer boxes are 18" deep, and I used 18" bottom-mounted glides.

tip

Door and drawer heights are commonly 1" greater than the opening height. The width is also 1" larger than the inside dimension of the cabinet using full overlay hidden hinges. If the stile edge to stile edge dimension is smaller than the side-to-side panel dimension, use the smaller distance.

There are many options available when selecting a drawer and door style. They can be as simple as a ¾" sheet of plywood or particleboard veneer with wood edge tape. Or you can build them as I have, in a five-piece raised-panel cope-and-stick style. These multipanel five-piece faces are made using a cope-and-stick as well as a raised–panel bit in a table-mounted router. The bit sets are expensive but will pay off in savings if you plan to make a lot of doors. The bit manufacturers provide instructions, but some general rules apply. The first cut to make is the cope on the end of both rails. The stick cut along the rail-and-stile edges then produces a clean cut at the ends with minimal tear-out. The normal stile-and-rail width is about 2¼". That dimension allows a hidden hinge to be mounted and leaves enough room for the decorative stick cut. Each bit set is different, so general rules for rail width before the cut cannot be given. I add 1" to my rail widths to achieve the required door width. The panel-raising bit cuts solid wood in different patterns and reduces the edge to about ¼", to fit in the door-frame grooves.

25 | Install the 18" bottom-mounted drawer glide members on the box and cabinet. Follow the manufacturer's instructions for glide positioning and alignment.

26 | Cut the rails and stiles to size based on your bit set. The finished size for the doors and drawer faces are detailed in the Materials List.

27 | Form the raised panel or use a ¼"-thick sheet of veneer plywood for your drawers and doors.

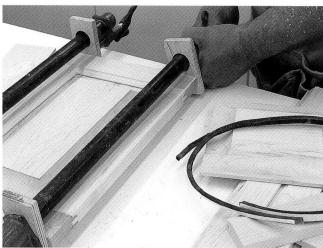

28 | Assemble the door and drawer faces. Use glue on the cope-and-stick joints allowing the panel to float when expansion and contraction of the wood takes place. I use a soft piece of inexpensive foam weather stripping to stop any rattles from loose center panels.

29 | Install the three drawer faces with 1" screws driven from inside the drawer box. Space the faces ¾" above the base shoe moulding.

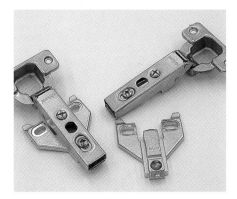

30 I set up my cope-and-stick bit set to cut a rabbet on the stiles and rails so it can receive a glass panel. If your bit set can't be modified you'll have to make a rabbet cut with a straight router bit. Order a ⅛"-thick glass panel for your door. The glass door frame is mounted with a standard 107° hidden hinge. The hinge mounting plate for this application is designed to fit on the face frame. This face frame mounting plate must be used because the stiles are further inside the cabinet than the cabinet sides. Drill two 35mm holes in the doorframe and mount the door. Many face frame mounting plates will align the door correctly with small locating tabs.

31 Cut two veneer particleboard shelves Z for the upper right section. Apply wood edge tape to the front edge and check the fit.

32 Drill a hole in the television section for power and antenna cables. Decorative hole grommets can be installed to hide the sheet core. Notice that I have the wood edged shelf Y installed in this illustration. I attached the hardwood edge to the front for added shelf strength in order to support any heavy equipment that will be installed. The television that is now occupying that section, as shown at the front of this chapter, is tall and would not fit with the shelf. In this case the shelf could be used for VCRs and remote control devices. Keep the shelf handy because the next television you buy may not be as tall, and this shelf could be used.

construction NOTES

I used ¾" maple veneer particleboard but any ¾" sheet material can be used. Special attention was paid to the load that would be placed on the television section, which is why hardwood cleats were added under the middle shelf.

The cabinet dimensions can be altered to suit your needs. Change the length, width or height to fit the space you have available.

I installed a quartz light bar in the glass door section to brighten the deep cabinet space. A light can also be installed in the right, upper section and I suggest you use tempered glass shelves. If you have a number of valuable pieces to display you might also want to add a glass door on the right end section as well.

Dividers can be installed in the drawers if you want to use them for thin articles like compact discs. Locks can be installed on the drawers if you require a secure storage area.

There are dozens of design options possible for this style of cabinet. A swivel mechanism can be used under the television, pocket doors to hide the TV could be installed, or the glass door could be replaced by a solid door so that section could be used as a bar. Don't hesitate to experiment with a few ideas to create your own special cabinet.

curio cabinet

One of the design challenges with a delicate project like this curio cabinet is how to make it sturdy while maximizing the display area. There is a great deal of glass involved and it must be properly supported. If you have valuable items to display, this is the cabinet of choice.

I DECIDED TO START WITH two solid 2×2 pieces of hardwood for the front corner posts, but square posts would not be very appealing and would look bulky.

I believe I solved the "big and bulky" look by creating a concave face on each post. It looks complicated, but in reality making the curved posts is a simple woodworking procedure.

The next issue I faced was finding a safe design to support large glass panels. The solution was to use a cope-and-stick style panel — two are fixed and the third became a door by installing hinges. This is a common method used to create frames for glass doors and proved to be just as suitable as a fixed panel frame. If you haven't yet purchased a cope-

and-stick bit set, this project is a good reason to buy one.

I'll discuss the many style options available to trim your cabinet. Subtle style changes in the trim can give the cabinet a totally different look. Investigate the style of your existing furniture to determine the final look of your curio cabinet. Look closely at the decorative wood details so that you can duplicate them on your cabinet.

Janice and Michael Bowie of Ottawa, Ontario, own the collection of world travel souvenirs shown here.

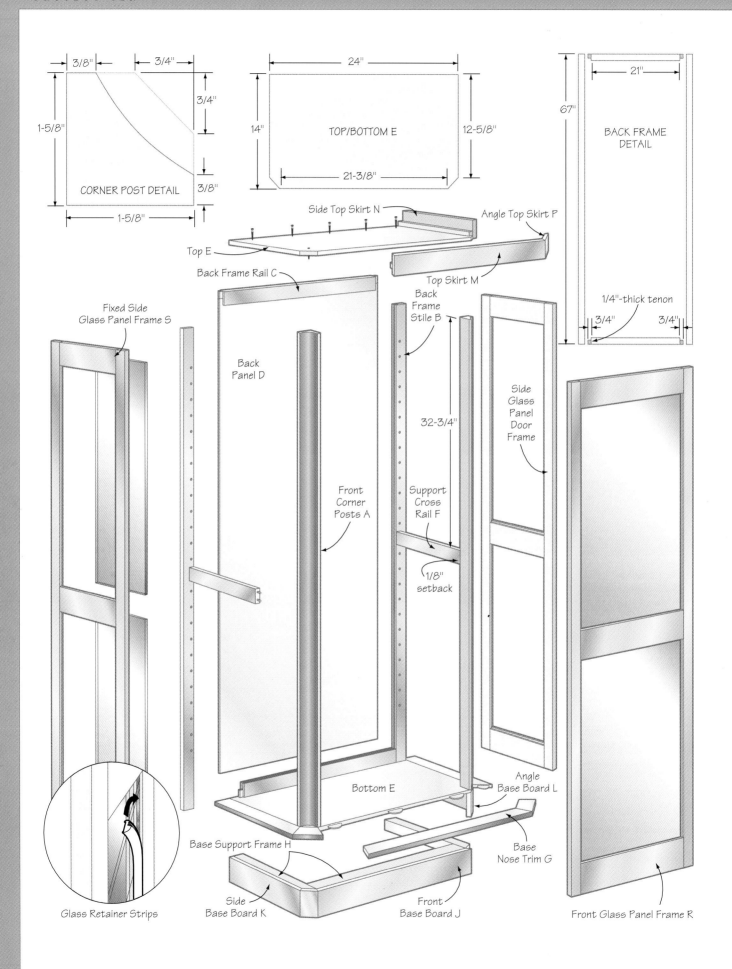

CORNER POST DETAIL

3/8" 3/4"
3/4"
1-5/8"
3/8"
1-5/8"

TOP/BOTTOM E

24"
14"
12-5/8"
21-3/8"

BACK FRAME DETAIL

21"
67"
1/4"-thick tenon
3/4" 3/4"

Side Top Skirt N

Angle Top Skirt P

Top E

Back Frame Rail C

Top Skirt M

Fixed Side Glass Panel Frame S

Back Frame Stile B

Back Panel D

Side Glass Panel Door Frame

Front Corner Posts A

32-3/4"

Support Cross Rail F

1/8" setback

Glass Retainer Strips

Bottom E

Angle Base Board L

Base Support Frame H

Base Nose Trim G

Side Base Board K

Front Base Board J

Front Glass Panel Frame R

materials list | **inches**

REFERENCE	QUANTITY	PART	STOCK	THICKNESS	WIDTH	LENGTH	COMMENTS
A	2	front corner posts	oak	$1^5/8$	$1^5/8$	67	angle cut & groove as detailed
B	2	back frame stiles	oak	$3/4$	$1^1/2$	67	
C	2	back frame rails	oak	$3/4$	$1^1/2$	23	
D	1	back panel	veneer ply g1s*	$1/4$	$22^1/2$	$65^1/2$	*good one side
E	2	tops & bottoms	oak	$3/4$	14	24	angled corner cuts as detailed
F	2	support cross rails	oak	$3/4$	$1^1/2$	$11^1/2$	
G	1	base nose trim	oak	$3/4$	$1^1/2$	60	cut into sections as detailed
H	1	base support frame	oak	$1^1/2$	$1^1/2$	50	cut into sections as detailed
J	1	front base board	oak	$3/4$	$3^1/2$	21	angle cut on both ends
K	2	side base boards	oak	$3/4$	$3^1/2$	$12^3/4$	angle cut on one end
L	2	angle base boards	oak	$3/4$	$3^1/2$	2	angle cut on both ends
M	1	top skirt	oak	$3/4$	$3^1/2$	22	angle cut on both ends
N	2	side top skirts	oak	$3/4$	$3^1/2$	13	angle cut on one end
P	2	angle top skirts	oak	$3/4$	$3^1/2$	$2^1/2$	angle cut on both ends
Q	1	top trim moulding	oak			60	angle cut to match top skirt boards
R	1	front glass panel frame	oak	$3/4$	$20^3/4$	67	
S	2	side glass panel frames	oak	$3/4$	$11^1/2$	67	one will be cut to provide door gap
T	6	frames & door panels	glass	$1/8$			cut to size required
U	6	shelves	glass	$1/4$			tempered with polished edges

*One-good-side plywood

materials list | **millimeters**

REFERENCE	QUANTITY	PART	STOCK	THICKNESS	WIDTH	LENGTH	COMMENTS
A	2	front corner posts	oak	41	41	1702	angle cut & groove as detailed
B	2	back frame stiles	oak	19	38	1702	
C	2	back frame rails	oak	19	38	584	
D	1	back panel	veneer ply g1s*	6	572	1664	*good one side
E	2	tops & bottoms	oak	19	356	610	angled corner cuts as detailed
F	2	support cross rails	oak	19	38	292	
G	1	base nose trim	oak	19	38	1524	cut into sections as detailed
H	1	base support frame	oak	38	38	1270	cut into sections as detailed
J	1	front base board	oak	19	89	533	angle cut on both ends
K	2	side base boards	oak	19	89	324	angle cut on one end
L	2	angle base boards	oak	19	89	51	angle cut on both ends
M	1	top skirt	oak	19	89	559	angle cut on both ends
N	2	side top skirts	oak	19	89	330	angle cut on one end
P	2	angle top skirts	oak	19	89	64	angle cut on both ends
Q	1	top trim moulding	oak			1524	angle cut to match top skirt boards
R	1	front glass panel frame	oak	19	527	1702	
S	2	side glass panel frames	oak	19	292	1702	one will be cut to provide door gap
T	6	frames & door panels	glass	3			cut to size required
U	6	shelves	glass	6			tempered with polished edges

*One-good-side plywood

1   The two front corner posts A are made with 2×2 stock from the lumberyard. In most areas the dressed size will be 1⅝" square. If your supplier doesn't dress to this size, order posts with the correct dimension. Cut one corner, along the full length of each post, at 45° on the table saw. Be sure the cut is ¾" in from the corner being removed.

3   The back frame is made with ¾"-thick stock and each of the four pieces has a ¼"-wide by ¼"-deep groove centered on the inside edge. These stiles and rails B and C are 1½" wide. The rails require tenons centered on each end to join the frame. Cut the grooves and tenons on a router table or table saw.

2   The angled face of each post is passed over the saw blade against a guide set at 30°. This guide bar is clamped in place and correctly positioned with the miter slide set at 30°. The post must be centered on the saw blade for the final cut to produce the correct cove cut. Follow the alignment procedures as some saw blades travel in an arc, as opposed to straight up and down, when the blade is raised. First, set the blade ¼" above the table and draw a reference line at the blade's center. Find the center of the angled face on each post and draw a line. Lower the blade and hold the post center line to the blade center line while positioning and locking the guide bar in place. Any error in positioning will be corrected during the final pass. Raise the blade 1/16" and make the first pass on each post. Repeat this procedure by raising the blade slightly and making slow passes across the blade. The cut is at the correct depth when the remaining edges of the angled faces are ⅜" wide. Check both edges after each pass, and when one edge is at ⅜", reverse the direction of feed. In other words, run the opposite side of each post against the guide bar during the last cut. This will ensure that each arc is centered on the angled faces of the posts. Finally, sand both posts to remove any saw marks.

4   Cut the back panel D and assemble the frame. The panel rests in the grooves and the frame is glued and clamped until the adhesive sets up. I used G1S (good one side) veneer for my panel; however, if you plan on installing a mirror use a less expensive ¼"-thick back panel.

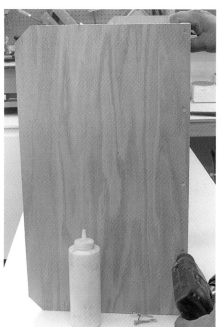

5 Prepare the bottom and top boards E by cutting them to the size shown in the Materials List. Place your posts on the front corners to determine the angle and dimension of the corner cuts. My cut dimensions are shown in the drawing, but you should verify the distances with your posts. Make the corner cuts on both top and bottom boards.

6 Attach the upper and lower boards to the back frame using glue and 2" screws. Drive the screws through the top and bottom boards into the frame, making sure its back edge is flush with the back edge of both bottom and top boards.

7 The front posts can now be attached. Using glue and 2"-long screws, drive through the top and bottom boards to secure the posts. Match the small, straight edges on each post arc to the edges of the top and bottom boards.

8 The side openings have two support cross rails F installed to strengthen the frame. Position the rails so their in-side faces are flush with the inside edges of the back panel stiles. Remember that the front posts are $1\frac{5}{8}$" wide so set the cross rail $\frac{1}{8}$" back from each post's inside edge. The top edges of the rails are $32\frac{3}{4}$" below the top edge of the front posts and back frame stiles. Fasten the rear end of each cross rail with a 2" screw. Don't use glue in case you decide to install a mirror on the back frame at a later date. The cross support's rear screw can be removed so the mirror will slide by the rail. The rear end of the cross support on the fixed panel side can be glued in addition to the screw. The front ends of these cross supports are secured to the front posts with dowels and glue. Again, verify the cross support lengths before cutting because your cabinet may differ slightly from mine.

tip

Attach temporary blocks to the bottom board at the same angle as the small corner trim boards. Clamp the boards using these temporary blocks until the pieces are secure.

9 | The base nose trim G is a 1½"-wide piece of wood that has been rounded over on the front edge. Use a ⅜"-radius roundover bit in your router to ease the front upper and lower edge of this trim before cutting to length. You'll need about 60" of material. The joints are mitered at 22.5°. The two side and front pieces are secured with glue and biscuits. The top edge of this trim is set flush with the top face of the bottom board. The two small angled pieces are secured with glue and clamps.

10 | The baseboard support frame H is made with 1½"-square lumber. Set the frame back 2¼" from the front edge of the nose trim. Cut the angles on the support frame boards at 22.5° following the nose trim line. Secure the boards with glue and 2" screws.

11 | Secure the base boards J, K and L, using glue and screws through the back side of the base support frame. Glue and face nail the two small angled base boards L in place. My base boards are plain, but you can cut any design into these boards with your router. Once again, the measurements I've given in the Materials List may differ slightly from yours so verify all dimensions before cutting the angles.

12 The top skirt M will be made with 3½"-high boards and applied moulding. You'll need about 60" of skirt board. Before cutting to length, use glue and nails to attach a ¾"-thick by 1"-wide cleat to the back side of the skirt board. This cleat is positioned ¹³⁄₁₆" above the bottom edge. It will be used to secure the skirt boards to the top of the cabinet, and will position the skirt ¹⁄₁₆" below the bottom face of the top board.

13 Attach the top skirt boards N and P using glue and brad nails. The joints are mitered at 22.5° to follow the outside edge of the top board.

14 Sand the skirt boards smooth and round over the bottom edge. Use a ¼"-radius roundover bit in your router to cut the edge.

15 The top trim moulding Q is a decorative element. Its design should be based on your taste and existing furniture. I used a flat moulding with a nose detail to match the bottom nose edge. This is a commercially available design, which can be purchased at many lumber stores. Attach the trim with glue and nails or screws. My trim is thick, so I can drive 1¼"-long screws from the back side of the skirt boards. You'll need about 60" of moulding.

16 The door and two fixed glass frame panels R and S are made with a cope-and-stick router bit set. The front will be a fixed glass panel frame, as will the left side. The right side will be a door which is built in the same style and using the same methods. The 67" panels and door require a center rail for support. This rail needs a cope cut on each end, as well as a stick cut on both edges. Measure your openings and cut the panels slightly oversize so they can be sized with a plane for a snug fit. The cope-and-stick bit set I use can be changed to cut a rabbet, in order to receive the glass panel. Cut all the pieces required to build the three panels. Use the offsets for your cutter set to build the panels with the final dimensions shown in the Materials List. There are two important steps before you begin making the panels. First, take accurate measurements of the openings on your cabinet. Second, make the stiles 1¼" wide and the rails 3" wide. These dimensions will maximize the viewing area.

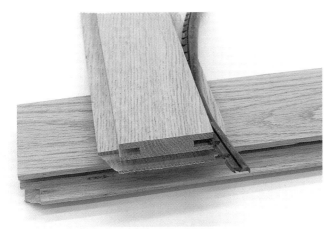

17 The next step before assembling the panels is to cut a groove for the rubber glass retaining gasket. Use a table saw to make the cuts. The groove is ⅛" wide and ⅛" from the inside corner of the rabbet cut. This type of retainer gasket is a press fit and does an excellent job of holding the glass in place. The glass retainer gasket is available at woodworking and hardware stores that carry door-making supplies.

18 Assemble the panels and door frames using glue and clamps. The middle rail on each assembly should be located at the center of each frame, and will cover the support cross rails.

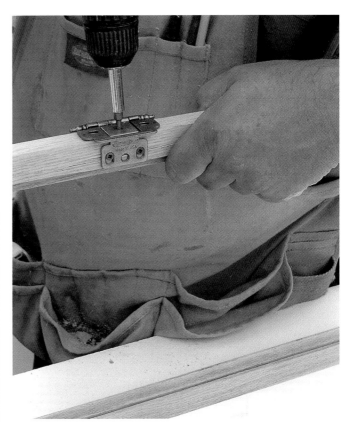

19 Install the fixed front and left side frames using glue and clamps. The face of the frames should be flush with the front edges of each corner post. The left side panel is flush with the outside edge of the back frame, as well as the edge of the front post. The frames are difficult to clamp tightly because of the arc in the front corner posts. One way to avoid having to clamp the frames tightly is to make them fit as snugly as possible. Size them carefully with your plane or sander to achieve that tight fit. Once the glue is applied and the frames are positioned correctly, clamp them lightly until the adhesive cures.

20 The door frame should be about ⅛" less in width and height than the opening. The gap should be as small as possible without binding. Mortise three hinges into the door or use the non-mortise hinge that I used. The hinges are attached 7" from the top and bottom, and the middle hinge must be offset to clear the cross support rail, as detailed in the next step.

21 The center hinge must be mounted above the door center line to clear the support cross rails. Determine the position by holding the door in place. Drill pilot holes for the screws and mount the hinge. Check the door gap and plane or sand as required to equalize the gap on all four edges. The door can be held closed by small magnetic latches that can be installed after the finish has been applied. Choose a door handle that matches the hinges.

22 Make an adjustable shelf hole jig that's ¾"-wide by ½"-thick. Drill equally spaced holes in the jig about 1¼" apart with a drill bit that matches the diameter of shelf pins you will be using. Then use the jig to drill eight columns of holes; four in the upper and lower back frame stiles and four on the back side of the front posts. A dowel rod can be used on the drill bit to limit the hole depth. Be sure to clamp the jig at the same position on each stile and post.

23 Measure and order ⅛"-thick glass panels for the fixed frames and door. You'll also need ¼"-thick tempered glass shelves with polished edges. Order as many shelves as required to suit your collection.

construction NOTES

I finished my cabinet with three coats of semi-gloss polyurethane. This finish matches the furniture in my house, however you can stain yours to match any décor.

There are a number of options for the door and fixed panels. A cope-and-stick bit set, along with the rubber gasket, is one of the best options because both sides of the frames are visible. However, you can make a simple frame, joined with biscuits or mortises and tenons, if you don't have a cope-and-stick bit set. The back edges will require a rabbet for the glass, and it can be secured with clips.

The cabinet width and depth suit my requirements but your needs may be different. Change the cabinet dimensions as required and follow the step-by-step construction.

When I completed the finishing I installed an 18" dual halogen lamp assembly behind the upper frame rail. Lighting adds the final touch to this beautiful cabinet and, because of the glass shelving, floods the interior to highlight your collection.

The cross support rails provide support to the cabinet. They can also be used to support one of the glass shelves, so take this into account when calculating the number and spacing of shelves.

Finally, install the handle and magnetic latches, shelf pins and glass shelves. All you need now is an interesting collection to complete the project.

military memorabilia cabinet

This cabinet is designed to display antique or collectible historical military equipment. It is the perfect cabinet for nonoperating arms that are sought after by many collectors. I would not store fully operational rifles or handguns in this display cabinet because I don't believe it has the required security, although it does include a lock.

THE UPPER SECTION IS FITted with racks, and the lower cabinet has an angled viewing platform. However it can be easily modified for other collectibles. For example, the cabinet could be used to display antique swords and knives, golf irons, old canes or baseball bats and souvenirs. The list is as long as are the needs for the different types of collections that require specialized storage and display.

This project was built using ¾"-thick veneer oak plywood and solid wood. Plate joinery, or biscuit joinery, is used to secure the face frame and mitered glass doors. Dadoes and rabbet joints have been used to assemble the casework.

The trim details do not add to the strength of this cabinet but simply enhance the appearance. The trim you use is a matter of personal choice, so substitute your favorite style to fit your décor.

This project features two storage drawers, but one large drawer might better suit your needs. The drawer boxes are made with Baltic birch cabinet-grade plywood using simple rabbet joinery. If you prefer a drawer box that's a little fancier, use hardwood and finger or dovetail joinery. This is another area that depends on your needs and choice, as well as your level of woodworking skill.

This is a specialized display cabinet that's fun to build. The collection of military equipment shown here is owned by Andrew Weston of Ottawa, Ontario. Mr. Weston is an avid collector and participates in historical battle reenactments.

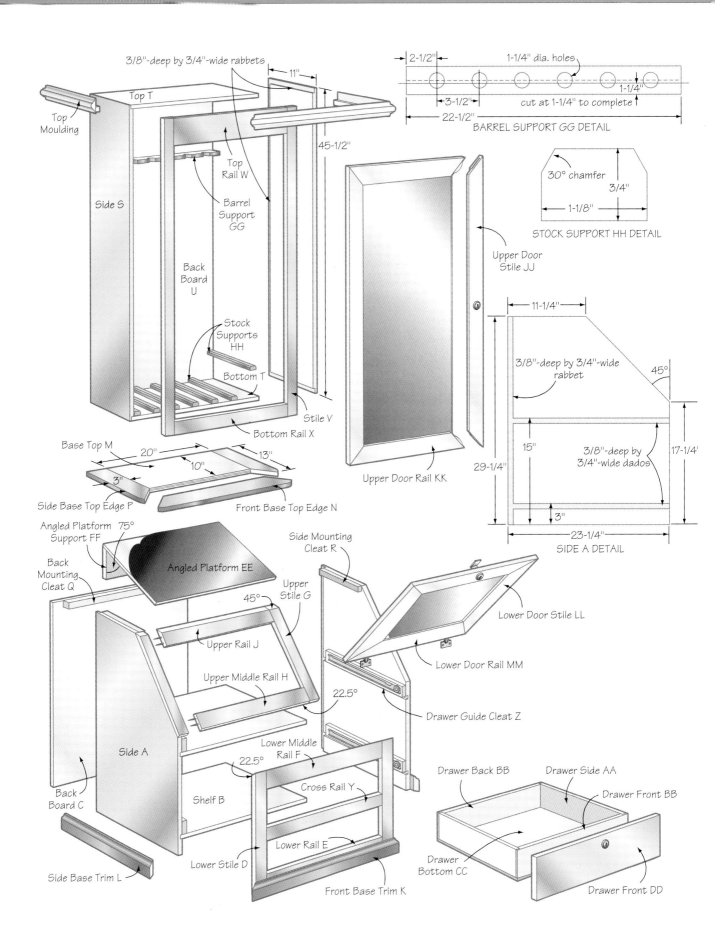

3/8"-deep by 3/4"-wide rabbets

11"

Top Moulding

Top T

Top Rail W

Side S

45-1/2"

Barrel Support GG

Back Board U

Stock Supports HH

Bottom T

Stile V

Bottom Rail X

2-1/2"

1-1/4" dia. holes

3-1/2"

1-1/4"

22-1/2"

cut at 1-1/4" to complete

BARREL SUPPORT GG DETAIL

30° chamfer

3/4"

1-1/8"

STOCK SUPPORT HH DETAIL

Upper Door Stile JJ

11-1/4"

3/8"-deep by 3/4"-wide rabbet

45°

15"

3/8"-deep by 3/4"-wide dados

17-1/4"

29-1/4"

3"

23-1/4"

SIDE A DETAIL

Upper Door Rail KK

Base Top M

20"

13"

10"

3"

Side Base Top Edge P

Front Base Top Edge N

Angled Platform Support FF

75°

Back Mounting Cleat Q

Angled Platform EE

Side Mounting Cleat R

Upper Stile G

45°

Upper Rail J

Upper Middle Rail H

22.5°

Lower Door Stile LL

Lower Door Rail MM

Drawer Guide Cleat Z

Side A

Lower Middle Rail F

22.5°

Cross Rail Y

Drawer Back BB

Drawer Side AA

Drawer Front BB

Back Board C

Shelf B

Lower Rail E

Drawer Bottom CC

Lower Stile D

Front Base Trim K

Drawer Front DD

Side Base Trim L

materials list | inches

REFERENCE	QUANTITY	PART	STOCK	THICKNESS	WIDTH	LENGTH	COMMENTS
Base Section							
A	2	sides	oak	$\frac{3}{4}$	$23\frac{1}{4}$	$29\frac{1}{4}$	
B	2	shelves	oak	$\frac{3}{4}$	$22\frac{1}{2}$	$23\frac{1}{4}$	
C	1	back board	oak	$\frac{3}{4}$	$23\frac{1}{2}$	27	
D	2	lower stiles	oak	$\frac{3}{4}$	$1\frac{1}{2}$	$17\frac{5}{8}$	
E	1	lower rail	oak	$\frac{3}{4}$	3	21	
F	1	lower middle rail	oak	$\frac{3}{4}$	$3\frac{1}{2}$	21	
G	2	upper stiles	oak	$\frac{3}{4}$	$1\frac{1}{2}$	$17\frac{1}{2}$	
H	1	upper middle rail	oak	$\frac{3}{4}$	$1\frac{1}{2}$	21	
J	1	upper rail	oak	$\frac{3}{4}$	3	21	
K	1	front base trim	oak	$\frac{3}{4}$	$1\frac{1}{2}$	$25\frac{1}{2}$	
L	2	side base trim	oak	$\frac{3}{4}$	$1\frac{1}{2}$	$24\frac{3}{4}$	
M	1	base top	oak	$\frac{3}{4}$	10	20	
N	1	front base top edge	oak	$\frac{3}{4}$	3	26	
P	2	side base top edges	oak	$\frac{3}{4}$	3	13	
Q	1	back mounting cleat	oak	$\frac{3}{4}$	1	$22\frac{3}{4}$	
R	2	side mounting cleats	oak	$\frac{3}{4}$	1	10	
Upper Section							
S	2	sides	oak	$\frac{3}{4}$	11	$45\frac{1}{2}$	
T	2	top & bottom boards	oak	$\frac{3}{4}$	$10\frac{1}{4}$	$23\frac{1}{4}$	
U	1	back board	oak	$\frac{3}{4}$	$23\frac{1}{4}$	$45\frac{1}{2}$	
V	2	stiles	oak	$\frac{3}{4}$	$1\frac{1}{2}$	$45\frac{1}{2}$	
W	1	top rail	oak	$\frac{3}{4}$	$3\frac{1}{2}$	21	
X	1	bottom rail	oak	$\frac{3}{4}$	$1\frac{1}{2}$	21	
	1	top moulding				40	
Two Drawer Option							
Y	1	cross rail	oak	$\frac{3}{4}$	$1\frac{1}{2}$	21	
Z	4	drawer glide cleats	oak	$\frac{3}{4}$	2	$21\frac{1}{2}$	
AA	4	drawer sides	Baltic brch	$\frac{1}{2}$	$3\frac{1}{4}$	22	
BB	4	drawer fronts & backs	Baltic brch	$\frac{1}{2}$	$3\frac{1}{4}$	$19\frac{1}{2}$	
CC	2	drawer bottom	Baltic brch	$\frac{1}{2}$	20	22	
DD	2	drawer fronts	oak	$\frac{3}{4}$	$5\frac{3}{4}$	22	
Angled Base Platform							
EE	1	platform	fir plywd	$\frac{1}{2}$	20	22	
FF	1	platform support	oak	$\frac{3}{4}$	5	22	
Upper Section Supports							
GG	1	barrel support	oak	$\frac{3}{4}$	$2\frac{1}{4}$	$22\frac{1}{2}$	
HH	7	stock supports	oak	$\frac{3}{4}$	$1\frac{1}{8}$	$10\frac{1}{4}$	
Door Frames							
JJ	2	upper door stiles	oak	$\frac{3}{4}$	$2\frac{1}{4}$	$41\frac{1}{2}$	
KK	2	upper door rails	oak	$\frac{3}{4}$	$2\frac{1}{4}$	22	
LL	2	lower door stiles	oak	$\frac{3}{4}$	$2\frac{1}{4}$	$13\frac{3}{4}$	
MM	2	lower door rails	oak	$\frac{3}{4}$	$2\frac{1}{4}$	22	
	2	panels	glass				

materials list | millimeters

REFERENCE	QUANTITY	PART	STOCK	THICKNESS	WIDTH	LENGTH	COMMENTS
Base Section							
A	2	sides	oak	19	590	743	
B	2	shelves	oak	19	572	590	
C	1	back board	oak	19	597	686	
D	2	lower stiles	oak	19	38	448	
E	1	lower rail	oak	19	76	533	
F	1	lower middle rail	oak	19	89	533	
G	2	upper stiles	oak	19	38	445	
H	1	upper middle rail	oak	19	38	533	
J	1	upper rail	oak	19	76	533	
K	1	front base trim	oak	19	38	648	
L	2	side base trim	oak	19	38	629	
M	1	base top	oak	19	254	508	
N	1	front base top edge	oak	19	76	660	
P	2	side base top edges	oak	19	76	330	
Q	1	back mounting cleat	oak	19	25	578	
R	2	side mounting cleats	oak	19	25	254	
Upper Section							
S	2	sides	oak	19	279	1156	
T	2	top & bottom boards	oak	19	260	590	
U	1	back board	oak	19	590	1156	
V	2	stiles	oak	19	38	1156	
W	1	top rail	oak	19	89	533	
X	1	bottom rail	oak	19	38	533	
	1	top moulding				1016	
Two Drawer Option							
Y	1	cross rail	oak	19	38	533	
Z	4	drawer glide cleats	oak	19	51	546	
AA	4	drawer sides	Baltic brch	13	82	559	
BB	4	drawer fronts & backs	Baltic brch	13	82	496	
CC	2	drawer bottom	Baltic brch	13	508	559	
DD	2	drawer fronts	oak	19	146	559	
Angled Base Platform							
EE	1	platform	fir plywd	13	508	559	
FF	1	platform support	oak	19	127	559	
Upper Section Supports							
GG	1	barrel support	oak	19	57	572	
HH	7	stock supports	oak	19	29	260	
Door Frames							
JJ	2	upper door stiles	oak	19	57	1054	
KK	2	upper door rails	oak	19	57	559	
LL	2	lower door stiles	oak	19	57	349	
MM	2	lower door rails	oak	19	57	559	
	2	panels	glass				

1 Cut the two lower side panels A to size. The front edge of each requires a 45° sloped face, as illustrated in the drawing. Building an angled panel cutter is the simplest and safest method for making the cut. These panel cutters are nothing more than a sheet of ½"-thick plywood with a ¾"-thick hardwood runner. The runner tracks are parallel to the blade in the miter slide groove. I have three of these handy panel cutters with fixed guide bars set at 22.5°, 45° and 90° to the blade. Make the sloped face cut on each side panel following the dimensions shown in the illustration.

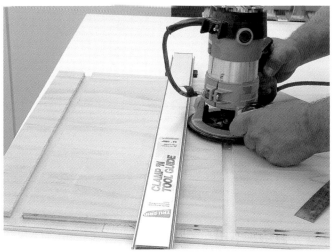

2 Both lower side panels require two dadoes and a rabbet on the inside face. All of the cuts are ⅜" deep and ¾" wide. Normally, I would use a ½"-thick back board, but I want the extra security and strength that a full ¾"-thick veneer plywood back provides. Use a guide bar and ¾"-diameter router bit to complete the cuts, as detailed in the drawing. Secure the shelves B in the dadoes using glue and clamps. Position each shelf so the front edges align flush with the front edges of the side boards. Install the back board C in the side board rabbets, and secure with glue and finishing nails. The top edge of the back board is aligned flush with the side board top edges.

3 The two lower stiles D are attached to the cabinet case with biscuits and glue. The top end of each is cut at 22.5°. Attach only one side at this time, and clamp it in place. The other side is dry fitted so the rails can be attached.

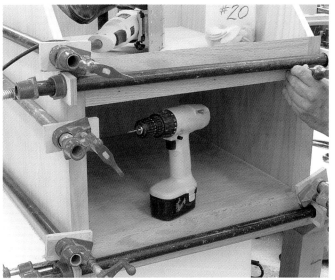

4 The lower rail E and lower middle rail F will be secured with biscuits and glue. The lower rail is 3" high and flush with the top face of the bottom board. The lower middle rail is cut at 22.5° on the top edge to align with the cut on the stiles. Use biscuits and glue to secure the two rails and remaining stile that were dry fitted. Finishing nails and glue can also be used to attach the rails to the fixed shelves, as the drawer face will hide the holes. Fill the nail holes with colored putty that matches the final finish.

5 The frames can be built as a one-piece unit and installed. Pocket-hole joinery can also be used to assemble the frames instead of biscuit joinery. Dowels or mortise-and-tenon joints are also good joinery options for face frames. The lower edge of the upper middle rail H, as well as both lower stile ends, are cut at 22.5°. The upper edge of rail J and upper ends of the stiles G are cut at 45°. Verify your cabinet case dimensions before making the final angle cuts on all the frame parts.

6 Attach the upper base face frame to the cabinet carcass. The top of the frame can be screwed to the cabinet sides with screws through the stile ends. A base top will hide these screws, but be sure to counterbore the hole so the screw heads are below the surface. This frame is difficult to clamp because of the angled edge on the cabinet, but there are a couple of techniques that can be used. First, both middle rails can be held together using small clamps hooked to a pipe clamp across the case. The round bar of the pipe clamp will allow the small clamps to be positioned at the correct angle. The stiles can be held tightly to the cabinet edges by driving a wedge under a "C-clamp" that is attached to the cabinet side boards. These wedges can be made by sanding thin strips of wood at an angle. Drive the wedges with a hammer until you begin to see the adhesive squeeze out.

7 The base trim K and L is made using 2"-high hardwood. A decorative cut can be formed on the top outside face with a router bit. I've used a Roman ogee bit, but any style will work. Attach the trim with glue and 1¼" screws driven from the back side. The corners are mitered at 45°. Remember to drill pilot holes before installing the screws to avoid splitting the trim.

8 Round over the outside edges of both base frames using a ⅜"-radius router bit. The base trim will limit the router travel so the remaining edge is eased with sandpaper. The base top extends beyond both cabinet sides and front by 1". The top M, N and P, is made with ¾"-thick veneer plywood and a 3"-wide hardwood edge. The hardwood is attached to the plywood with glue and biscuits. Both front corners are joined with 45° miters.

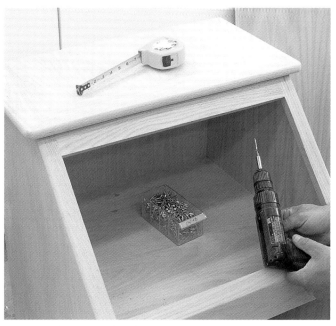

9 Attach the three mounting cleats Q and R flush with the top edges of the cabinet carcass. Use glue and brad nails or screws to secure the cleats. To secure the top, predrill holes in the cleats for the screws. Round over each front corner with a belt sander to remove square corners. Use a ⅜"-radius roundover bit to ease the front top and bottom, as well as the top and bottom side edges, with your router, then sand smooth.

10 Attach the completed top to the cabinet base with glue and 1¼"-long screws, using the predrilled holes in the mounting cleats. The back edge of the top should be flush with the back face of the back board.

11 The two upper side boards S require three rabbet cuts to accept the top, bottom and back boards. These rabbets are ⅜" deep and ¾" wide. Form the rabbets using a hand-held router and guide or use a router mounted in a table. Cut and join the upper section top and bottom boards T, and the back board U, to the sides. Use glue and finishing nails to secure these panels in the rabbets. The nails can be driven from the top and bottom into the side panels, and through the back board into the sides. Check the diagonals of the carcass to make sure it's square. A properly cut back board will ensure the carcass is squared as you install the panel.

12 The face frame for the upper section is made with ¾"-thick solid wood. The outside dimensions are 24"-wide by 45½"-high. I have joined the rails W and X to the stiles V with pocket joinery and glue. Biscuits, dowels or mortise-and-tenon joints are all perfectly acceptable as well.

13 Attach the face frame to the upper section carcass using biscuits and glue. The top edge of the frame should be flush to the upper face of the top board. The outside edges of the frame should be flush with the outside faces of the side boards.

14 Sand the face frame and round over the outside edges of each stile using a ³⁄₈"-radius roundover bit. Begin rounding at the bottom and stop ³⁄₄" short of the top end.

15 The upper section is attached to the base section using 1¼" screws. Align the top section so it's flush with the base at the back, with equal spacing on each side.

16 I used a moulding with a rounded face that is a favorite of mine. If possible, attach a mounting cleat to the back of the trim. Nails can be driven through the trim into the top of the cabinet carcass to avoid face nailing. Miter the corners at 45° and install the trim ¾" down from the top edge of the cabinet using glue and brad nails.

17 The base section can accommodate one large deep drawer or two smaller drawers. The number of drawers you make depends on your storage requirements. My needs called for two smaller drawers, so I installed a middle rail Y to equally divide the space, using pocket screws and glue. It can also be installed with small wood cleats or metal brackets and glue. This rail is primarily decorative, but will act as a stop for a lock that will be installed.

18 The Blum bottom-mounted drawer glides must be installed flush with the inside dimension of the drawer opening. The inside dimension of this cabinet space is the stile-to-stile measurement. The cabinet sides are set back and therefore require cleats to align them with the inside stile edges. Cut the four drawer glide cleats Z using ¾"-thick material. I used some of the veneer plywood from the sheets used to build the carcass. Attach the cleats with glue and nails at the bottom of each drawer opening.

19 The drawer box width and height is 1" less than the drawer space. Therefore, the boxes must be 3¾"-high by 20"-wide; I used the standard 22"-deep size. Then I used ½"-thick cabinet-grade plywood, sometimes called Baltic or Russian birch, to make my drawer boxes. Both ends of each drawer side require a ½"-wide by ¼"-deep rabbet to attach the front and back boards. Cut the drawer parts as detailed (or calculate the sizes if you've chosen the one door option) and attach the sides to the front and backs with glue and brad nails. Install 22" bottom-mounted drawer glides and test fit the drawer boxes. Follow the manufacturer's instructions when installing the glides.

20 My drawer fronts for this project are simple hardwood boards with the front face edges rounded over. Use 1" screws to attach the drawer face to the box. If you've chosen your handle or knob, drive a screw through the drawer face hole securing it to the drawer box when it's aligned properly. Then gently open the drawer and drive screws through the box into the back of the drawer face.

21 The base section display compartment should have an angled platform for better viewing of your collectibles. Cut a piece of ½"-thick plywood, and a rear support cut with a 15° angle on the top edge. I will be covering this platform with felt and leaving it loose in the compartment so it can be removed for cleaning.

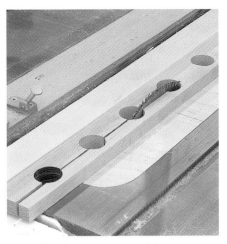

22 The barrel support GG is a series of half circles cut through a piece of hardwood. Drill six 1¼" holes about 3½" apart, or at a distance to suit your collectibles, through the hardwood.

23 Cut the support on a table saw to create the half holes. Set the width at 1¼" so a good portion of the hole diameter remains in the support.

24 Attach the barrel support to the back wall of the upper case. The position will be determined by the requirements of your collectibles. Use 1¼"-long screws through the rear face of the back board to secure the support.

25 The stock supports HH for the upper section are glued and nailed to the bottom board. Each support is chamfered at 30° on both top edges using a table saw. This cut is for decorative purposes only. Space the supports about 2¼" apart, starting with one support placed against each side board. Your requirements may be different so this setup is an example of one option. I used 2¼"-wide stiles and rails to build the doors. The corners were joined with 45° miters using No. 10 biscuits and glue. Cut all the pieces to size, then clamp securely until the adhesive sets.

26 Sand both frames smooth, then round over the inside and outside front edges on both doors. Use a ⅜"-radius roundover bit to ease the edges. I used a ⅛"-thick slot-cutter bit in my router table to form a rabbet on the back inside perimeter of both doors. The ⅛" depth was chosen to match the ⅛"-thick glass that will be installed. Square all the corners after cutting the rabbets with a sharp chisel.

27 The glass can be secured in the rabbets using many methods. A wood strip is one option. A plastic or metal clip also works well. I used a plastic clip, available at your local hardware store or glass supply shop. Ask to see a selection of fasteners when you order the glass.

28 Drill two 35mm-diameter holes in each door, ⅛" from the edge. My hinge holes are set 4" from each end. I used Blum series compact hinges because they work very well with this type of glass door.

29 Attach the hinge plates to the face frames with ⅝"-long screws. Drill a pilot hole before installing the screws to avoid splitting the wood. The compact face frame hinge plates have stops on the outside edge for easy alignment. Push the stops against the outside edge of the face frame and install the screws.

30 Install barrel locks on both doors and each drawer. These locks are available at local hardware stores and provide some security for your collection.

construction NOTES

After completing a final sanding I removed all the hardware and applied three coats of polyurethane. The final coat was hand rubbed with #0000 steel wool and a small amount of clear paste wax to achieve a smooth finish.

The removable platform was covered with felt, and the glass was installed using plastic clips as discussed in step 27.

I also installed small, round low-voltage lights in both sections. The light switch is an in-line type attached to the power cord. I routed the cord behind the cabinet and positioned the switch for easy access.

There are a number of door options throughout this book that can be used on this cabinet. The formal mitered corner style used on these glass doors is popular and very elegant looking, so it's a great choice for this cabinet.

I doubt that everyone will have the same display requirements for their collections. A number of uses for this cabinet have been suggested by people visiting the shop including baseball equipment, golf clubs and mementos, antique tools and weapons, swords and so on. I'm sure I heard up to twenty possible uses for this collectibles cabinet. All those possibilities mean that you will most likely have to design specific supports for both the upper and lower sections of your collection.

Complete the cabinet by installing locks and appropriate handles or knobs. It's an interesting project with a number of challenges, but it is one of my favorite cabinets in the book. I enjoyed building this project and I'm sure you will as well.

sources

There have been many suppliers who have contributed products, material and technical support during the project building phase of this book. I appreciate how helpful they've been and recommend these companies without hesitation.

ADAMS & KENNEDY
Manotick, Ontario
613-822-6800
wood supply

DELTA MACHINERY
800-223-7278 (in US)
800-463-3582 (in Canada)
www.deltawoodworking.com
woodworking tools

EXAKTOR PRECISION WOODWORKING
Markham, Ontario and
Lewiston, NY
800-387-9789
www.exaktortools.com
table saw accessories

HOUSE OF TOOLS
Edmonton, Alberta
800-661-3987
woodworking tools
and hardware

JESSEM TOOL CO.
Penetanguishene, Ontario
800-436-6799
www.jessem.com
Rout-R-Slide and
Rout-R-Lift

PORTER-CABLE
Jackson, TN
800-487-8665
www.porter-cable.com
woodworking tools

RICHELIEU HARDWARE
Ville St. Laurent, Quebec
800-619-5446 (in US)
800-361-6000 (in Canada)
www.richelieu.com
hardware supplies

ROCKLER WOODWORKING AND HARDWARE
Medina, MN
800-279-4441
www.rockler.com
woodworking tools
and hardware

TENRYU AMERICA
West Melbourne, FL
800-951-7297
www.tenryu.com
saw blades

TOOL TREND LTD.
Concord, Ontario
416-663-8665
woodworking tools
and hardware

VAUGHAN & BUSHNELL MANUFACTURING
Hebron, IL
815-648-2446
www.hammernet.com
hammers & other tools

WOLFCRAFT NORTH AMERICA
Itasca, IL
630-773-4777
www.wolfcraft.com
woodworking hardware

WOODCRAFT
Parkersburg, WV
800-225-1153
www.woodcraft.com
woodworking hardware

WOODWORKER'S HARDWARE
Sauk Rapids, MN
800-383-0130
woodworking hardware

index